KU-495-682

Independent Living for Adults with Mental Handicap:

'A Place of My Own'

Margaret C. Flynn

With a Foreword by Professor Robert B. Edgerton

CASSELL

Cassell Educational Ltd
Artillery House, Artillery Row
London SW1P 1RT

Copyright © Margaret C. Flynn 1989

All rights reserved. No part of this publication may be reproduced or transmitted in any form or by any means, electronic or mechanical including photocopying, recording or any information storage or retrieval system, without prior permission in writing from the publishers.

First published 1989

1589130

British Library Cataloguing in Publication Data

Flynn, Margaret C.
  Independent living for the mentally handicapped:
  a place of my own
  1. Mentally handicapped persons.
  Community care.
  I. Title
  362.3'58

  ISBN 0 304 31474 9

Phototypesetting by Fakenham Photosetting Ltd, Fakenham, Norfolk
Printed and bound in Great Britain at
The Camelot Press Ltd, Southampton

Contents

Acknowledgements

This book owes a great deal to the 88 people I met who are living independently and their support personnel. The people I interviewed shared their experiences willingly and always made me welcome in their homes. I hope this book will be of use to them and to the people who follow them.

The research on which this book is based was funded by the Economic and Social Research Council (1983–86) at the Hester Adrian Research Centre, University of Manchester. The Joseph Rowntree Memorial Trust provided additional funding to write this book. During the course of the research I have been fortunate to have had the advice and encouragement of Professor C. Kiernan, Professor R. Parker, Dr J. Hogg and Dr N. Raynes.

The research could not have taken place without the help of six social services departments. I am grateful to Mr C. Kirk, Mr Howard Lomas, Mr Mike Cunningham, Ms Rachel Lomas and Ms Sally Pugh of Bury Social Services; Miss I. Walton, Mr Godfrey Travis, Miss Betty Barraclough, Mrs Anna Fedecko, Ms Olwen Gourley, Mrs Frances Smith, Mr George Topping and Mr Tim Teehan of Manchester Social Services; Mr R. Lewis, Mr Richard Woolrych, Mrs Sue Griffiths, Ms Clare Gormanley, Mr Martin Haigh and Mr John Ryan of Oldham Social Services; Mr. V. J. P. Scerri, Mr Phil Dand, Ms Clara Flemming, Ms Jean Murray and Ms Sylvia Williams of Salford Social Services; Mr J. G. Poyner, Mr Jack Hulme, Mr Matt Brown, Ms Irene Fairhurst, Mrs Jocelyn Gombos, Mrs Brenda Griffiths, Mrs Pat Gunn, Miss Barbara Headland, Ms Josie Howarth, Ms Marie Kelly, Mr John Siddall, Mrs Pat Tither, and Mrs Pam Yates of Wigan Social Services; Mr Se Queira, Mr Rickard, Mr D. Gurr, Mr Ken Fitton, Mr Ken Griffiths, Mrs Irene Hunt, Mrs Mairs, Ms Chris O'Dowd, Ms Frances Roberts, Mr Keith Scregg, Mrs Angela Stansfield, Mrs Joy Southworth, Mr Tim Sullivan, Ms Jean Whitfield, Mrs Wickham and Mrs Ann Wilson of Wirral Social Services. Thanks are also extended to Mrs Maureen Douglas of Salford Mental Handicap Case Register. Collaboration with all of these people was of inestimable value.

I have been lucky to have had the support, advice and encouragement of Dr Elizabeth Byrne. She has been influential in the planning of the research and this book. Her interest and enthusiasm have been invaluable. Mr David Reeves has advised on the analysis of this research throughout the three years. The interest and support that he provided, particularly during the final phase, contributed a great deal to this research.

Ms Christina Knussen and Ms Jannat Saleem patiently undertook to establish the reliability of some of the measures used in this research. Mr Keith Cornelius, Ms Eila Kielty, Christina Knussen and Ms Hazel Qureshi read, advised and commented on the initial draft of this book. Their recommendations, along with those of the anonymous Cassell reviewers, resulted in significant improvements. Dr Elspeth Bradley, Ms Frances Brown, Ms Louise Goodbody, Miss Stella Hall, Dr Elinor Kelly, Howard Lomas, Mrs Vicky Martin, Ms Chris McKenna, Mr Ron Pardoe, David Reeves, Ms Jane Ritchie, Jannat Saleem, Dr David Towell and Sylvia Williams provided valuable feedback on the final section.

Lastly, thanks are extended to Ms Leslie Sellars who transcribed some 30 interviews and to Ms Judith Toon and Ms Pat Mellor who assisted with the typing.

Foreword

Professor Robert B. Edgerton

Ever since the earliest studies of mentally handicapped people who were released from institutions began to appear early in this century, it has been clear that substantial numbers of these people – usually a majority – have been able to live more or less independent and troublefree lives in community settings. It is now possible to say with considerable confidence that most mildly and even moderately mentally handicapped persons can make a satisfactory adjustment to life outside of institutions if they are given enough time to do so and if they have the support of other persons.

This is a very positive finding, but it can also be an illusory one, for it masks the difficulties and suffering that many individuals experience as they struggle to find a life and place of their own. In recent years, investigators in several parts of the world have begun to look more closely at the processes by which mentally handicapped people adapt to the demands of community living. Increasingly, mentally handicapped people have been allowed to speak for themselves about their hopes, and their fears, their triumphs and their failures. Studies such as these have permitted us to see the lives of mentally handicapped people as these people themselves see them, to appreciate the problems they face, and to understand better what needs to be done if society is to help them along the road to independence. Through such intimate research we can also learn that mentally handicapped people have much that they can offer to society. To take a single case in point, as mentally handicapped people grow older, they sometimes need more and more assistance coping with the everyday problems of life, but paradoxically many of these people grow so much in strength and maturity that they become important resources for others. By looking beneath surface appearances and by allowing mentally handicapped people to describe their worlds as they experience them, we can avoid reaching stereotypic conclusions that serve neither their needs nor those of society at large.

Dr Margaret C. Flynn's book, *Independent Living for the Mentally Handicapped: 'A Place of My Own'*, is a welcome contribution to our knowledge about the lives of mentally handicapped people. She has listened to the voices of 50 men and 38 women, many of whom are growing older, as they spoke about their lives.

What they have said to us is often touching but sometimes painful as, for example, when we learn how often they are poor, lonely and victimized by others. Dr Flynn skilfully marshals the evidence of their lives as they see them, building a balanced portrait of them as people with skills and with needs. Perhaps most powerfully she shows how these mentally handicapped people are often ill-served by hospitals and social service agencies. With details that will be familiar to readers in the United States as well as the United Kingdom, she shows us again and again how great is the need for training in skills required for independent living and how lacking are job opportunities and suitable housing.

Some of Dr Flynn's most important and original findings have to do with the vital role that social workers can and must play in at least the early stages of learning to live independently, what an important role social skills play in community living, and how functional it is for mentally handicapped people to have structured routines of daily living. She also trenchantly describes deficiencies in existing policies that overlook and reinforce poverty, make personal victimization more likely to take place, and provide too few residential alternatives. These doleful findings are hardly confined to the men and women Dr Flynn tells us about. They are widespread in many industrialized societies, including the United States.

Perhaps the greatest value of Dr Flynn's book lies in its specific recommendations that, if heeded, would bring social service providers much closer to meeting the needs of mentally handicapped people. For this she deserves our gratitude, and for allowing us to hear once again what it is like to be poor, socially isolated and vulnerable yet hopeful of better times to come, we are doubly in her debt.

Professor R. B. Edgerton
Department of Psychiatry
University of California
Los Angeles

Part 1

The background to independent living for adults with mental handicap

1

Perspectives on Independent Living

During an in-service training programme for practitioners working with people with mental handicap, a woman recalled a dilemma she had experienced. Her brother James, who has a mental handicap, had lived with his grandmother for many years. When his grandmother became ill and had to go into hospital, this woman told her brother that there were two options: 'You can either go into a hostel, or move in with me and Bill until grandma's better.' James replied, 'I want to stay where I am.'

This incident encapsulates the caution that attends independent living for people with mental handicap. Families and services do not readily acknowledge that continued residence in a house and locality with which a person is familiar and known, is an option to be considered. Although James's sister lost some sleep over her brother's decision, he regarded the patch of independence as unremarkable and was bewildered by his sister's frequent and unannounced visits.

In this book the lives and circumstances of 88 people with mental handicap are described. Nine people have never lived in any form of staffed accommodation but have continued to live in their former family homes. The remainder have lived in hospitals and hostels, sometimes for vast periods of their lives. The fact that these people currently have their own front-door keys and have all been living in their homes for over a year reflects a number of recent policy commitments: small living arrangements are recognised as being preferable to large; people with mental handicap should not be placed in hospitals; and community-based living arrangements should exist.

People who live in hospitals and hostels have attracted the lion's share of research attention. In contrast, people who live in their own homes have received scant attention. In this country, the reason for this neglect may relate to the fact that the number of people with mental handicap living in their own homes is small (Department of Health and Social Security Personal Social Services Local Authority Statistics, DHSSPSSLAS, 1977–82). Perhaps the situation reflects the widespread underexpectation that plagues this population. If we do not believe that people with mental handicap ever attain adult status, with all the benefits that this implies, then there is little reason to promote their independence and even less reason to evaluate it. One of the aims of this book is to begin to redress the balance.

This chapter outlines briefly the background to independent living for adults with mental handicap in this country. A consideration of development in the growth of services is followed by an overview of the influential philosophy of care, 'normalisation'. Lastly, the picture that emerges from American research regarding people leaving hospitals and the contributions of research originating from Britain, are presented.

DEVELOPMENTS IN THE GROWTH OF SERVICES

Over a number of years there have been significant developments in the growth of services for adults with mental handicap. The initiative for these has come from government reports, legislation, changes in social policy, philosophies of care and research findings. As good accounts of the developments in the growth of services have been published elsewhere (Alaszewski, 1986; Malin, 1987; Raynes, Sumpton and Flynn, 1987), this section constitutes no more than a summary of these.

 • *Better Services for the Mentally Handicapped* (DHSS, 1971) recommended the following: a move to community care for 35,000 people in hospital; the development of small-scale domestic facilities promoting individualised services; the end to segregation; and the involvement of health, local authorities, voluntary and private organisations in the development of alternative residential provision.

 • The United Nations Declaration of the Rights of Mentally Retarded Persons (1971) acknowledged that people with mental handicap have been treated as outcasts and denied the range of opportunities available to other people. Although the existence of a clear statement of rights is no guarantee that there will be no deprivation of these, the absence of a bill of rights in this country means that there is no possibility of protecting rights through litigation.

 • A report of the Committee of Enquiry into Mental Handicap Nursing and Care (Jay, 1979) outlined three general principles: the right to enjoy normal patterns of life within the community; the right to be treated as individuals; and the need for additional help from the communities in which they live. This position was developed by the King's Fund Centre paper (1980) *An Ordinary Life* and the Independent Development Council for People with Mental Handicap (1981) which concluded that services should

> . . . affirm and enhance the dignity, self-respect, and individuality of mentally handicapped people who are people first and mentally handicapped second; pay due regard to what mentally handicapped people and their families want and be informed by their views; enable them to share in and contribute to community life, including family life, and to assist them to lead as normal a life as possible, where necessary providing extra help to enable them to do so.

• The National Development Group for the Mentally Handicapped (1980) published a checklist of standards highlighting the need to ensure that people with mental handicap are entitled to the same range and quality of services as others.

• *Care in the Community*, a DHSS (1981) consultative document promised new financial arrangements to help people with mental handicap living in hospitals to move into the community and therefore make redundant the large, old institutions. Subsequently Circular HC (83)b (DHSS, 1983) was issued enabling district health authorities to make annual payments to local authorities and voluntary organisations for people who were leaving hospitals.

• The Second Report from the Social Services Committee 1984–85 (House of Commons, 1985) observed that the 'almost obsessive concentration in public policy on the mechanisms for "getting people out of hospital" has sometimes obscured the basic fact that most . . . mentally handicapped people already live in the community'. Among the resulting 101 recommendations, the following are especially pertinent to people living in their own homes:

1 . . . There is a general and growing groundswell of opinion which is questioning the way in which so-called community care policies are operating in practice. The evidence . . . and the range of anxieties and reactions revealed suggest strongly that Parliament must find means of giving greater and more regular consideration to . . . mental handicap policies. (paras 27–29)
2 . . . The Minister must ensure that . . . mental handicap hospital provision is not reduced without demonstrably adequate alternative services being provided beforehand both for those discharged from hospital and for those who would otherwise seek admission. (paras 30, 40)
4 . . . It is vital that the pressing problems confronting those mentally disabled people already living in the community be more fully taken into account in developing policies of community care. (para 24)
6 We recommend that the Department lay an obligation on authorities to ascertain as far as practicable, and give due consideration to, the wishes and feelings of mentally disabled individuals for whom a service is provided, and in particular where closure of a long stay hospital is contemplated. We also recommend that efforts be made to facilitate the participation of individual mentally disabled people in the planning and management of services. (para 149)
We are at the moment providing a mental disability service which is underfinanced and understaffed both in its health and social aspects. We recommend that the Government now accept that genuine community care policies are achievable only in the context of some real increase over a period of years in expenditure on services for mentally handicapped . . . people. (para 21)
41 Service planners at all levels must be aware that the need for daytime occupation is not limited to 9 to 5, Monday to Friday. Facilities of some sort must be available during evenings and weekends, and the cost implications of such a service have to be taken into consideration in planning for community care. (para 80)

• The Disabled Persons (Services, Consultation and Representation) Act 1986 made provision for a disabled person and/or their representative to be consulted about services. The person and/or their representative may make representation concerning their needs, may be supplied with information, and may attend meetings or interviews held by an authority concerning services that affect them. Further, a local authority is obliged to take account of difficulties in communication on the part of the disabled person or their representative. Although the Act was passed in the knowledge that it would have a phased implementation, this has been progressively delayed because of concerns regarding resource implications.

From holding an excessively medicalised view of people with mental handicap, regarding them as passive recipients of care, policies have moved on to recognising them as potentially active partners in improving services. The extent to which this is a reality for the population whose lives are the focus of this book may be judged from the following chapters.

NORMALISATION AS A PHILOSOPHY OF CARE

Normalisation has had considerable impact on services for people with mental handicap. Rarely is a job advertised in this field without some reference to the philosophy. It grew from efforts to improve services for people with mental handicap and it is based on the proposition that the quality of life increases as access to culturally typical activities and settings increases.

The term was coined by Nirje (1969) who defined it as 'making available to the mentally retarded patterns and conditions of everyday life which are as close as possible to the norms and patterns of the mainstream of society' (p. 181). Deceptively simple, the stress for change was aimed at service providers.

Normalisation was reformulated by Wolfensberger (1972) for implementation in American society. He defined it as, 'the utilization of means which are as culturally normative as possible in order to establish and/or maintain personal behaviors and characteristics which are as culturally normative as possible' (p. 28). Thus the emphasis was switched from the service providers to the individual, the goals becoming the adjustment and maintenance of behaviours which are as typical or as 'normal' as possible (Race, 1987).

Normalisation developed from the belief that societies reject some people because of their difference. In turn, this led to the relegation of people with disabilities into poor-quality, segregated settings. It is acknowledged that the philosophy of normalisation laid the groundwork for the implementation and evaluation of deinstitutionalisation efforts (Willer and Intagliata, 1984).

The philosophy has not been spared criticism. Holbrook and Mulhern (1976) proposed that a superficial understanding of normalisation may lead to the development of poor-quality services. Similarly McCord (1983) reported that service personnel generally hold a limited view of normalisation. He found that staff ignored the impact of social norms and values in dealing with people with mental handicap. Concern has been expressed that according to normalisation, contact with peers with mental handicap should be limited (Rhoades and Browning, 1977). Some researchers saw normalisation as an attempt to make people normal at the expense of their individual differences (Aanes and Haagenson, 1978; Hendrix, 1981).

Flynn and Nitsch (1980) pointed out that human services have demonstrated an 'adoption in theory' rather than an 'adoption in practice' of normalisation. The premise that normalisation involves an attempt to treat everybody, regardless of their disabilities, as full human beings tends to be overlooked.

In 1983 Wolfensberger gave normalisation a new name: social role valorisation. This reflected his conviction that the paramount aim of normalisation is the creation, support and defence of valued social roles for people who are at risk of devaluation. Bayley (1988) sees a flaw in the revamped philosophy and contends that what is valued or normal in a particular culture is debatable. Vash (1982) observed:

Members of groups targeted for exclusion are persuaded, and society at large is convinced, that for them to play certain roles is 'unnatural', 'inappropriate', or 'impossible'. Little girls are taught to become nurses, not doctors; vocational rehabilitation clients must entertain only 'feasible' (low-cost, low-risk) goals; black, disabled and female students are forgiven, not pushed, when mathematics and science concepts are difficult for them; and we are all prepared early to expect deterioration and yield our employment rights when we become old. (p. 16)

Are these the social roles for which we are preparing people with mental handicap and are they desirable? Bayley proposes that the ultimate goal of social role valorisation, emphasising independence rather than interdependence, may be unhelpful for this population.

To the extent that Wolfensberger (1983) saw the promotion of social role valorisation being accomplished by two major subgoals – the enhancement of people's social image, and the enhancement of people's perceived competencies – the lives of the 88 people I met reflect the philosophy of social role valorisation. As most adults, they have their own homes and their living arrangements mostly reflect their preferences. In the main, people have been prepared for their independent lifestyle, and with assistance it is being sustained. However, it will be seen that the extent to which these people have valued social roles in the localities in which they live is open to debate.

There is undoubtedly a widespread concern about people with mental handicap leaving hospitals and hostels. Is it in people's best interests to remain in a protected environment with familiar surroundings, with people they know who have cared for them, sometimes for decades, despite the knowledge that institutions are often justly berated for their inadequacies? Or should people be transferred to community-based, smaller-scale environments where they may have the opportunity to live independently? Research goes some way to addressing these concerns.

LEARNING FROM RESEARCH: THE AMERICAN PERSPECTIVE

Residential services for people with mental handicap have undergone dramatic change in recent years and a trend on both sides of the Atlantic is the reduction in the numbers of people in the large institutions. The consequences of people leaving institutions in the United States have been monitored from as early as 1919 by Fernald. More recently, McCarver and Craig (1974) summarised the findings of the large corpus of research concerning deinstitutionalisation and identified the factors that are associated with community placement 'success'. They noted no consistent differences in the community placement success rates of men and women or of people of different ages. There is no strong association with intellectual level, so it is not the most able people who are going to manage living in the community. Research on the influence of people's adaptive behaviour skills yields mixed results. It appears, however, that where preplacement behaviour problems are assessed, these are associated with community failure or poor adjustment. It should be noted that these research findings relate largely to the transfer of people with mental handicap from large-staffed to smaller-staffed institutions.

In a study of independent living, one of the characteristics of people for which fairly consistent relationships with community adjustment was found, is personal appearance (Gollay et al., 1979). Schalock, Harper and Carver (1981) also reported that personal care and clothing care are important predictors of placement success.

Landesman Dwyer (1981), Heller (1984) and Braddock and Heller (1985) advocated the need to consider carefully people's friendships before implementing a transfer to another residence. Disruption of people's relationships adversely affects their adjustment and is one of the best predictors of placement breakdown.

Many studies indicate that the experience of being relocated has deleterious effects on physical health and behaviour. If health is poor before a transfer, this is associated with stressful reactions to relocation. The expectations of the person with a mental handicap about the move also affect relocation. Some of the stressful reactions to being transferred may be moderated with support from friends, families and staff.

There is little doubt that a pertinent message of American research is that attempts to predict the adjustment of people with mental handicap on the basis of individual characteristics are futile. Community adjustment is a multidimensional and a highly complex process and the interaction of individual characteristics with environmental characteristics has to be the focus of attention. In spite of the call for consistent criteria of successful adjustment, Cobb (1972) made this observation about people who have left hospitals: 'The most consistent and outstanding finding of all follow-up studies is the high proportion of the adult retarded who achieve satisfactory adjustments by whatever criteria are employed' (p. 145).

The lessons from the powerful anthropological work of Robert Edgerton (1967) are especially relevant to this book. He investigated the lives of people with mild mental handicap who graduated from Pacific State Hospital habilitation programmes. He found that these people were ill-prepared for the complexities of daily living outside hospital. Many devised surrogate biographies excluding their years in hospital and attempted to develop non stigmatised self-images. People's central concerns hinged on making a living and making relationships with friends and lovers who had no connection with the hospital. Edgerton described people's attempts to 'pass' in order to appear normal, contending that they were preoccupied with avoiding confirmation of their incompetence to themselves and others. 'Benefactors' featured significantly in their lives, that is, non-mentally handicapped people who entered into a 'benevolent conspiracy' to help them to cope with independent living. Edgerton concluded that the 'cloak of competence' worn by the people he met failed them during times of personal and social crisis.

In a follow-up study, Edgerton and Bercovici (1976) reported that it was not possible to predict who would improve and who would deteriorate. Over time, it appeared that people were less stigmatised by their mental handicap and they were less concerned about deceiving themselves and others. Recreations, hobbies, friends and family made their lives more pleasurable and people saw themselves as normal, irrespective of their poor employment records and their earlier concern with this. A further follow-up by Edgerton, Bollinger and Herr (1984) showed that the importance of benefactors continued to diminish and people came to rely more on their own resources. They were committed to enjoying life, confident that they would manage and inspired by an 'unshakeable optimism' that their lot would improve.

In summary, American research points to the complexity of community adjustment. It suggests that it is achievable by people with mental handicap irrespective of their gender, age and IQ. Importantly, friendship networks have to be respected if transfers to community placements are to work. People who have transferred from institutions have few social and financial resources to draw from and they are especially vulnerable to personal crises. Over time, people depend on others less and their lives are more satisfying to themselves. It appears to be beyond human ingenuity to predict the course of a person's life.

LEARNING FROM RESEARCH: THE BRITISH PERSPECTIVE

Turning to Britain, the theory is that the resettlement of people with mental handicap from institutions into community settings is controlled by the rate of increase in community services and the availability of housing. A 'homelands' policy operates of returning people to the locality from which they came. In a survey of the closures of thirteen hospitals for people with mental handicap, Wertheimer (1986) observed that most people were moved to hospitals, national health service hostels and community units. Thus, the closure of the hospitals was largely achieved by moving people to other institutions. Some reservations have been expressed about the alternative forms of care which have developed with many of the characteristics of institutions (National Development Team, 1985).

The history of people with mental handicap being relocated into community settings is not extensive in Britain. The few studies pertaining to independent living are largely qualitative. In sum, they present a jigsaw of insights that parallel some of the findings of American research.

Mattinson (1970) and Craft and Craft (1979) studied the lives of married couples with mental handicap. They demonstrated that these people's lives are not vastly different from those of the rest of us. Mattinson in particular showed that people's former association with institutions was a painful subject.

Malin (1983) highlighted the fact that the selection of people for group living on the basis of skill, strengths and weaknesses, for example, is indefensible. Group harmony is recognised as being of key importance in determining eligibility to live in a group home. In a study of six group homes, Malin showed that people depended mainly on support provided through official networks. The main reason for the removal of individuals from the group homes was recurring, disruptive behaviour leading to opposition from other residents and support staff.

Atkinson (1980) proposed that 'independence' is something of a misnomer. Following a study of 50 people leaving hospital, she suggests that after the 'honeymoon' period, people's limited understanding of general life experience, means that they are likely to be dependent on '. . . a social worker, maybe a home-help, possibly on the local training centre and, almost certainly, on the Social Services Department'. Poverty impacts considerably on people's lives with most managing on 'a subsistence level'. Mindful of their tendency towards limited social contacts, Atkinson and Ward (1987) note, 'we have been slow to realise that helping people settle into ordinary houses in ordinary streets does not of itself bring integration into "the community" or a high quality of life . . . we have to look beyond the bricks and mortar, to ways of encouraging the development of social relationships in community settings'.

The above outline of research findings indicates that caution about the selection of individuals for group living is appropriate. People's friendships are important and should be maintained in spite of the 'homelands' policy. Formal support personnel feature significantly in people's lives. Overall, independent living arrangements are not easy options for people, not least because their incomes are limited and financial poverty is a theme in their lives.

SUMMARY

This chapter sets the scene for the remainder of the book. The prospect of people with mental handicap living independently raises many concerns. This is bound up with questions regarding their adult status and the inclination of families and service providers to be protective.

Influential documents resulting in service developments are highlighted. These chart the perception of people with mental handicap from passive individuals requiring medicalised care to potentially active partners in improving services. The growth of the philosophy of normalisation is outlined.

The contributions of research to our understanding of the process of relocating people from hospitals to community settings are summarised. Community adjustment is a highly complex process. It is not enough for researchers to look merely at the characteristics of an individual. We have to consider a person's life 'in the round'. It is not the most able people in terms of IQ who are going to manage an independent lifestyle. It is essential that people's friendships are carefully considered before relocation. Where preplacement behaviour problems are assessed, these are associated with postplacement problems. People's health may be adversely affected by relocation to another setting. People who have been relocated have few social and financial resources to draw from, and reflections on an institutionalised past are very painful to them.

2
The Development of the Community Placement Study

Several years ago I lived as a co-resident in a tenancy for four people, three of whom were described as having a mental handicap. Some months following my departure, local youngsters gained access and set fire to the tenancy. Although nobody was injured, extensive damage resulted and the three men concerned were returned to their former places of residence. The incident was the culmination of a sequence of hostile activities by young people (described in Flynn, 1984), and it prompted me to reflect upon the quality of the lives and circumstances of other people with mental handicap who live in their own homes.

At the beginning of 1983 I acquired an ESRC Postdoctoral Fellowship to undertake a study of independent living for adults with mental handicap. As it was a one-person research project, I focused on local authorities in North-West England.

Prior to the onset of the funding period (October 1983 to September 1986) I wrote to eleven directors of social services and requested their assistance. Their eleven local authorities were recorded in the Department of Health and Social Security Personal Social Services Local Authority Statistics (DHSSPSSLAS) as having unstaffed community places for adults with mental handicap. (The DHSSPSSLAS were subsequently found to be a wanting source of information as they vastly underestimated the numbers of people living in unstaffed tenancies; see Flynn, 1986a). Eight Directors of Social Services responded favourably to the prospective investigation and nominated 'link' persons with whom I met to discuss the study.

Following these discussions, one area was excluded from the study as it did not keep case records on its clients. The existence of case records was critical as they were an important source of information. While it is appreciated that some people with mental handicap live in their own homes and do not receive social work services, the identification of these people was beyond the scope and resources of this project. In the remaining seven areas, social services personnel were willing to participate in the study and they kept case records. One of these areas subsequently withdrew without explanation and six areas finally took part. These were spread throughout the North-West and included two inner city areas, three former mill towns and one area combining small industrial and rural towns.

The main purpose of the community placement study was to describe people's lives and circumstances in their own homes. To achieve this, the study was conducted in three phases: (1) the pilot study; (2) the main study; and (3) analysis of the data.

THE PILOT STUDY

In the first phase, three local authorities were selected from the DHSSPSSLAS (1977–82). The three areas demonstrated contrasting development in terms of their provision of unstaffed places for adults with mental handicap. In association with the 'link' persons, and practitioners supporting people living in their own homes, a number of issues were explored:

- Is it possible to measure 'successful' placements?
- How feasible is it to use the case records compiled by social services departments and community mental handicap teams as sources of information?
- How feasible is it to incorporate information gathered from interviews with people with mental handicap in material for subsequent analysis?

As a result of this phase it became clear that the lives of people with mental handicap living in their own homes were characterised by their diversity. No consensus on the features of 'successful' placements could be obtained. Case records were found to be neither homogeneous nor complete and differences in recording were evident within and between social services departments (see Sumpton, Flynn and Raynes, 1986). However, a good deal could be gathered about the course of people's lives by reference to their case records. Finally, following informal conversation with some fifteen people living in their own tenancies, I considered the perspectives of adults with mental handicap as too important and rich to omit. They were primary informants about their own lives.

At the end of the pilot study, four measures were devised and these were tested in one local authority.

(1) The *information from case records* measure organised and categorised the information generally available in case records about a person's history and current living circumstances. I completed this initially and it was subsequently checked and amended by the social worker.

(2) The *information from social workers* measure gathered details about the frequency and type of contact with the client; the person's skills, activities and income. It also gave social workers an opportunity to rate the success of their client's placements. (The time it took to complete the information from both case records and social workers did not impinge significantly on the work of the support personnel. This concern had been aired by directors of social services at the outset of the study.)

(3) The *house environs and living facilities* measure was completed by me following a visit to the people's homes. I noted the type of housing, home ownership, the existence of household belongings and facilities, local amenities and the rateable value.

(4) The *interview schedule* attempted to establish whether people could manage particular tasks alone and whether they were satisfied with such aspects of their lives as their daily activities and neighbourhoods, for example.

Where possible, an effort was made to introduce issues and concerns addressed in other studies of independent living for adults with mental handicap. The completed measures and a comprehensive account of their development appear in Flynn (1985a).

THE MAIN STUDY: COLLABORATION WITH SOCIAL SERVICES DEPARTMENTS AND COMMUNITY MENTAL HANDICAP TEAMS (CMHTs)

Primarily, phase two involved collaboration with social services and CMHT personnel and interviews with people in their own homes. In association with the 'link' person in each area, I contacted the personnel with responsibility for people living independently. The 34 personnel who completed both the information from case records and social workers measures included fifteen generic social workers, twelve specialist social workers, five home carers and two social work assistants. Thus in this book the term social worker describes a mixed group of people. Information about the extent of people's experience in working with people with mental handicap was not gathered.

The 'link' people, social workers and I randomly selected between ten and eighteen people in each area. Where there were more clients in a particular area than the number I wished to see, selection was made alphabetically. Two people were excluded from the selection process as their social workers were concerned about their mental illness and violence respectively.

At initial meetings with social services and CMHT personnel I described the aims and methods of the study. In order to complete the information from case records measure, I read each person's case record. Along with the information from social workers both measures were left with the social worker for checking and completion respectively. As I moved from one local authority to another, the practitioners who were involved in the study were kept informed of developments by means of regular project bulletins.

The interviews took place following advice from people's social workers about the most appropriate means of contacting their clients. Mostly people were approached by letter and asked if they would be willing to participate in the study. Many social workers contacted their clients beforehand, told them about the study and asked them if they wanted to take part. If people did not wish to be interviewed, it was made clear that no attempt would be made to encourage their reconsideration. In total, only one person declined to be interviewed. The resulting study population of 88 people consisted of those who agreed on their own behalf to be interviewed. Before the interviews started, I explained that nobody had to answer any questions if they did not wish to do so. This had also been specified in the contact letter. The majority of the interviews were taped. This was also presented as an option. Everybody was interviewed in their own home. A small number of people chose to have their social workers with them.

Particular attention was paid to ways of overcoming the difficulties inherent in interviewing people with mental handicap. The pilot study permitted prior knowledge of the communication skills of fifteen adults and it was clear that verbal interviewing techniques were generally applicable. During the interviews, topics were introduced during the course of conversation rather than in an inflexible sequence. All of the interviews were transcribed. Following each interview I made my own observations regarding the situation of the interviewee and his/her reaction to particular topics. These 'field notes' were used in rating people's satisfaction regarding homes and social contacts for example (see Flynn, 1986b for further details).

The last part of phase two consisted of telephone calls and visits to social services departments and community mental handicap teams to gather completed measures. All measures had been returned by April 1986.

ANALYSIS OF THE DATA

Phase three was concerned with the analysis of the information gathered from the four measures. It began with the preparation of data from the house environs and living facilities measure and the interview schedule. As information from these measures was not dependent upon checking, amendment or completion by social workers, it was coded and punched directly onto the mainframe computer. Information from the remaining two measures was coded and ready for analysis by May 1986.

The information gathered was analysed in four stages. Initially, frequency distributions or 'head counts' were calculated. In order to reduce this descriptive information, a number of areas of interest were identified: money; demographic details, health, hygiene and appearance; housing; interpersonal issues; daily and leisure activities; household tasks; placement; contact and support; locality; and success. Within each of these areas, indices were developed. An index combines several items or responses into a single measure and permits a more complex treatment of data. Next, the associations between indices were examined using Pearson Product Moment Correlations. The results of some of these appear in Appendix 1. Finally, a number of indices were selected as outcome measures. Outcome measures were selected to represent both positive and negative aspects of people's lives. Examples of positive outcomes include: 'success' as rated by social workers; and 'satisfaction' as described by the people interviewed. Examples of negative outcomes include 'victimisation' as noted in case records; and, 'concern' as expressed by families and professionals and noted in case records. A series of multiple regression analyses was carried out to see which factors were most closely associated with these outcomes. The results of these are presented in Appendix 2. These and additional findings, are reported in Chapters 4 to 8.

SUMMARY

This study took place in North-West England. I contacted eleven directors of social services whose local authorities were recorded in the DHSSPSSLAS as having unstaffed community places for adults with mental handicap. Eight directors responded favourably to the prospective study and 'link' people were nominated in each area. Ultimately the study took place in six areas.

A pilot study demonstrated that the lives of people with mental handicap living in their own homes were characterised by their diversity. No consensus on the features of 'successful' placements could be obtained. Case records were found to be a useful source of information. The information gathered from informal conversation with fifteen people living independently, demonstrated that they merited inclusion in the study as primary informants. Four measures resulted from the pilot study: information from case records, information from social workers, house environs and living facilities, and the interview schedule.

Collaboration with social services and CMHT personnel and interviews with people with mental handicap characterised the main part of the study. In each area, between ten and eighteen people were randomly selected. In the final phase of the study the information gathered was analysed. Firstly, in order to indicate differences and similarities among people living independently, frequencies were collated. To identify which people were vulnerable, a series of multivariate analyses were undertaken using indices that were arrived at by combining together all the responses to particular themes.

Part 2

People's lives and circumstances

3
People Living Independently: Different Lifestyles

The aim of this chapter is to provide a three-dimensional picture of the lives of nine people: three who live alone; three who live with partners; and three who live with two or more others.

The majority of the people I met manage in the community with varying degrees of assistance from social services and community mental handicap team personnel. (It will be recalled that all of the study population are known to social services departments or CMHTs.) The people whose lives are described here include those who are reliant on considerable help, those who receive moderate help, and those few who manage their affairs with little assistance. An attempt is made to present detailed accounts of the lives and views of individuals with contrasting skills, support networks and living circumstances. Apart from the information regarding people's appearance and their homes, most of the historical information was gathered from case records. People's names have been changed. For convenience, the historic present tense will be used.

THE PEOPLE

Miss Linda Mason

Miss Mason is a short and heavily built woman of 28 years. She has a speech impairment and pronounced facial asymmetry following a series of cleft lip and palate operations. In addition Miss Mason finds walking problematic as a result of her recent, considerable weight gain.

Although there is no record of Miss Mason's IQ profile, her social worker regards her as having a 'mild' mental handicap. As a youngster she left the family home at the request of her parents. She was acknowledged to be jealous of her sister who is physically very attractive. Miss Mason sought her mother's constant attention and was considered to be 'overprotected'. Although she had occasional outbursts of temper at home, these were always directed at inanimate objects.

Miss Mason initially lived in a specialist hospital and from this she moved to a hostel, where she lived for six years. During her stay in residential accommodation Miss Mason had operations associated with her cleft lip and palate. From the point of view of the staff, she was difficult to manage in so far as she ignored hospital instructions. She did not enjoy association with other residents, was sometimes verbally abusive and was frequently absent from the hostel without permission. In respect of family contact, Miss Mason went home regularly (she preferred to have baths in the family home). Behaviours that resulted in particular concern were Miss Mason's public displays of affection for her teddy-bear and occasional 'dummy' sucking. Away from her family, her unhappiness was so overwhelming that she wrote the following letter to the manager of her adult training centre (ATC): 'I am leaving you all for a time being . . . so it is no use looking for me or getting the pilleces cause I am going to find some way of dieing or kill myself as I am fed up. . .'.

Miss Mason moved into her own flat three years ago because 'she had proved successful in a hostel training unit'. The flat is in an attractive three-storey block in a quiet residential area. It is homely and comfortable and reflects Miss Mason's pride in her home and her housework. Her own brightly coloured abstract pictures adorn the walls. Drawing is one of her favourite occupations and she invests a lot of time in this.

Miss Mason left the ATC soon after moving into her flat and concern regarding the absence of structured daily activities has been expressed on her behalf:

'I got thrown out of the ATC. There was a bit of bother yer see, something got me annoyed. They complained about the way I was doing my job. I thought if they want to complain about me job, I'm not going to do anything.'

Miss Mason has days of strict routine. Her home carer photocopies a timetable of household tasks for her each week. This is unvarying and it is Miss Mason's preference:

'In the mornings I get up and make meself a drink . . . and I start me jobs, see what I have to do [by referring to timetable], and then I start. . . . If I don't go out I either do some writing or drawing or sometimes I watch TV, play some records and do some dancing. I might do a bit of singing. . . . When I get money, the first thing I do is get me stamps. I get gas, electricity, telephone, then TV. The second thing I do is I put £1 aside for me milk and the third thing I do is pay for me papers. And when I do that, I do me shopping and watch me money. Sometimes I try to save a bit if I can, but I very rarely do save but things are going up that much. I think it's terrible. That's all really. I don't do very much really.'

Miss Mason has £41 each week and although she has had some debts, she mostly manages her budgeting well. Miss Mason's home carer visits her weekly. He is helping her to diet by dieting with her. They both have weight charts in her flat and they are monitoring each other's weight loss. Miss Mason's home carer is encouraging his client to broaden her leisure interests and attend art classes. So far, she is not enthusiastic. Also, the home carer is counselling his client about contact with her neighbours and friends. He is concerned about her interpersonal difficulties:

> *'I like living on me own. I like this flat but the trouble is the neighbours are not nice with me. They won't let me be friends. I mean, that upsets me a bit. . . . They are always funny with me. . . . What I feel in the flat is that it's a shame when you can't get on with people and I don't really, you know. It's something I can't seem to help and I don't really know why. I mean when you can't go and see anybody and nobody come and see you, well you know the days seem to go longer and the nights seem to go longer as well. . . . John [boyfriend who is 30 years her senior] said he'd like to live with me. I said they won't let us. If he lived with me they'd take my money off us. That's what I got told anyhow you know. . . .'*

Throughout the interview Miss Mason cuddled her teddy-bear and whispered to it occasionally. She made it with the help of her grandmother whom she sees often. She visits her parents or they visit her at least once a week. She is concerned that she is unable to find open employment:

> *'I keep trying to get work. I've been to the Job Centre a few times but you see I can't read real writing, I can only read what's printed. So if I get any letters I can't read I just ask me social worker and ask me mummy when she comes.'*

Miss Mason's home carer regards his client as 'moderately successful' and wants her 'to continue to live in the community and become less dependent on professionals'.

Mr Raymond Carney

At 44 years Mr Raymond Carney leads a somewhat unsettled existence. Classified as having a 'moderate' mental handicap, he is also described as mentally ill. Mr Carney is one of four children. He had a stormy childhood during which he was exposed to the violence of his father, directed most frequently at his mother. In his early teens, following the death of his father, Mr Carney also became aggressive and violent towards his mother. This behaviour and his intermittent ATC attendance brought him to the attention of services, and at the request of his family he was placed in a hospital.

During Mr Carney's five-year residence in hospital he received psychiatric treatment. Contact with his family was sustained throughout this period and he was most anxious to return to the family home. Rehabilitation personnel felt that there were indications 'that some signs of stabilisation in Raymond's behaviour might be obtained through a combination of medication and social training'. Mr Carney returned home to live with his elderly mother. In the period prior to his mother's death, Mr Carney still had aggressive outbursts that were largely directed towards her. This resulted in cautions from the police and regular contact with the social services.

Mr Carney misses his mother and he recalled a conversation he had with a member of staff at an ATC he once attended:

'He said "I believe your mother's dead Raymond. I'm very sorry, it must get a bit lonely for you being on your own." I said "Yes, it does most of the time but you have to get over it. . . ." She was nice, I miss her. I wish I hadn't done that what I did . . . I used to knock her down. I didn't mean to do it. Does God punish people for that?'

Mr Carney lives in a small flat on an estate that is in decline. He is of average build and height and takes little care over his appearance. When I met him he had been living alone for over a year. Mr Carney became subdued when he reflected upon the contact he has with his family. He regrets that his brother does not wish him to go to his home:

'He helps from time to time . . . now and again he comes down on a Saturday to see me. . . . I've not never been to his house. . . . He doesn't like me most of the time.'

Mr Carney goes to see his social worker almost daily. He is annoyed that she does not visit him as often as he would like. In turn she is perplexed by the frequency of his visits and observed:

'Because of the amount of social work time given to Raymond during the periods he spends in my office, I made an agreement with him that if I were to visit him on a weekly basis it would not be necessary for him to visit the office. So far this has not proved to be workable and Raymond is still coming to the office.'

Boredom is a conspicuous difficulty for Mr Carney. Local ATCs will not offer him a place because of his erratic attendance and occasional violence:

'I've nothing to do. . . . I get bored because I've no ATC to go to. . . . I go on the market sometimes . . . I help people . . . I help at loading and things like that.'

Suggestions and encouragement to Mr Carney to look after himself, and his flat and to avoid unscrupulous individuals is regarded as a source of irritation:

'Me brother said for to sleep in me bedroom but I've never slept in a bed. I can't sleep. That's why I get on there [settee]. . . . Harry used to come and see me but he got me in debt. Me brother don't like him . . . I've been paying off a pound a week for to get rid of it.'

Mr Carney has few social contacts beyond those of his social worker and brother. His social worker believes that he cannot handle interpersonal relationships, and particularly relationships with women. Mr Carney's brother believes that Mr Carney should be in a hostel. In contrast, his social worker's main objective is 'to contain him in the community'. She describes her client as 'moderately successful'.

Mr Fred Payne

Mr Payne is a short and stockily built man of 54 years. Although there is no reference to his IQ in his case record, his social worker and other professionals associated with Mr Payne estimate that their client has a 'severe' mental handicap.

Mr Payne has always lived in his current neighbourhood. Following the death of his mother he continued to live in the former family tenancy. He came to the attention of the social services when a sibling notified them of the death of their mother. On assessment it was clear that Mr Payne was not coping adequately and that he was socially very isolated. Also, his home was in a poor state of repair and was due for demolition. In order to prevent further deterioration, Mr Payne was given daily support and once a tenancy became available, he moved. Some two years later, the daily support continues from the social services and the College of Further Education he attends, where he receives training in self-help and social academic skills. Although he says that college is 'all right', Mr Payne is dispirited that he no longer has a job.

> 'Can't get nothing now can yer? I were a labourer you know, loading waggons for a long while. Can't get a job nowhere, can yer? I haven't bothered since. It's all right getting one but it's them as gets in before you'.

When Mr Payne moved into his flat he experienced some intimidation from a neighbour. This person objected to Mr Payne having been allocated such a desirable tenancy. As a result of social service and housing department intervention, however, the taunting of the neighbour ceased. He currently has no contact with any neighbours.

Mr Payne lives in a modern, attractive, warm and very comfortable flat on a busy street. He has many photographs on display of his mother and family, and ornaments on most surfaces. He likes his flat and appreciates central heating:

> 'They knocked down the street where I lived. It was a council house but they got me into this. The council that . . . they've been good to me. Only a gas fire in the other one. . . . They've knocked a lot of old houses down round here you know. It's all changed now. The other street were quiet yer know.'

At college Mr Payne mixes freely with staff and students and he has a sense of humour that is described as 'ever ready'. Outside college, however, he has no friends and his most frequent visitors are social services personnel. At weekends he visits two sisters who live in the locality. They help him, although they require frequent reassurance that their brother can, and is managing. Social services personnel help Mr Payne most particularly with money management, looking after his health and hygiene, his home and household routines and with the management of his free time. Mr Payne budgets on £34 a week and commented, *'Social worker sorts that out see'*. As he is unable to read, he takes his letters to college, or to his sisters' or shows them to his home help or social worker. Of his general activities, Mr Payne commented:

> *'I go to college every day. I go Monday, Tuesday, Wednesday, Thursday, Friday. It's all right. . . . When I get in I just have a rest that's all. I watch TV all right. That's my radiogram that. I got it one Monday night that I got it. I had a record player before and I sold it. It's a good one. . . . I go to the pub at nine o'clock sometimes.'*

Mr Payne's social worker describes his client as 'successful' and wants Mr Payne to continue his existing lifestyle. He is concerned however that his client, 'could not function without the existing (daily) levels of home help input'.

Mr and Mrs Fraser

Mr and Mrs Fraser are both in their 50s and they have lived in their own flat for ten years. They met in a residential centre for people with epilepsy and Mr Fraser made his leaving conditional upon being with his partner. They married and initially moved into a co-residency.

All that is known of Mrs Fraser's family is that they requested her removal from the family home at an early age and they did not wish her to return. Nothing is known of her early experiences in residential care. Mr Fraser was an only child and his mother died when he was young. Concern was expressed by social and medical services when Mr Fraser attacked his elderly father. This violence, which recurred in combination with frequent absence from his family home, led to his compulsory admission to hospital. He was made the subject of a two-year probation order and he remained in hospital for a year. From here he moved to a specialist hospital and then to a centre for people with epilepsy. Mr and Mrs Fraser moved to a hostel, then to a co-residency and finally to their current joint tenancy.

Unlike his wife, Mr Fraser had a high profile during his residence in staffed accommodation. He experienced interpersonal problems with staff and residents and he was physically and verbally abusive. In staffed accommodation Mr Fraser received psychiatric treatment. Mrs Fraser did not enjoy association with staff and residents and, like her husband, was very keen to leave.

Mr and Mrs Fraser have a history of poor health. Mr Fraser has a metabolic disorder and has had a series of stomach operations. Latterly his employment has been terminated through illness. Mrs Fraser has a heart condition and as a result of this she has swollen legs which limit her mobility. Mrs Fraser's epilepsy is much more severe than that of her husband and she has had some serious falls as a result of these. Mrs Fraser is also subject to 'occasional psychotic episodes'.

Mr and Mrs Fraser did not like living in the co-residency. They did not get on with their co-residents and they wanted the privacy of their own home. Interpersonal difficulties still prevail for this couple. They do not get on very well with each other, and as a result of this and their health, they receive a great deal of support from their social worker. Both take a lot of medication and at least once a week, with their social worker Bill, they sort out their daily tablets and put these into separate envelopes. They have difficulties regarding their budgeting and, as they have had mail order debts, their financial transactions are supervised. A particular interest of this couple engages their social worker in an activity not generally acknowledged to be within the sphere of activities of social services personnel: the repair of radios, tape recorders and clocks. They both enjoy gadgets and they showed me their combined lighter/cigarette holders with undisguised pleasure. My continual surprise at the sheer volume of hourly noise from the chiming clocks was a source of considerable entertainment for them. Their clocks and tapes are an important interest. Mr Fraser explained:

'We've got the two little ones in town and they both chime. And that one comes from in town. We got the big one first but the end one there comes from Scarborough. And the next one, with gold on it, we got that one from town, but not from the same place the big one. I used to do a lot of taping. . . . I'm not so big interested in it really to a certain extent because I've that many you see.'

Mrs Fraser added, *'He's doing them for me.'* Mr and Mrs Fraser have family photographs in their sitting room. Mr Fraser explained that he had *'coloured them in'* and the effect was strange in their darkened room.

Mr and Mrs Fraser reflect carefully about managing their flat and their health, particularly in relation to epilepsy:

'I mean to say we manage . . . we just manage on us own. I mean if he can't do the cooking, I do it. There's not a lot to do really. We just do our shopping and that like. . . . Now I'll tell you one thing . . . now this might sound a bit comical to you . . . but if anybody starts mithering, saying 'is he all right' and the rest of it, it'll take me longer to come out of it . . . [epileptic fit] you see it would take us both all the longer to come out of it . . . the best really is to ignore you and leave you alone you see . . . if there's a lot crowded round you, you can't get no fresh air. . . .'

Their social worker is concerned that his clients have very limited social contacts, that Mrs Fraser is occasionally lonely, and that he is their only visitor. They live in a small flat on a quiet street and they do not know their neighbours. Mr Fraser said:

'If they don't bother with you, don't take no notice. It's best way . . . because they'll only start causing trouble you see what I mean. . . . There's only Bill comes to see us, there's nobody else. . . .'

Mr and Mrs Fraser are described as having a 'mild' and 'borderline' mental handicap respectively. Their social worker has known them and worked with them for twelve years and he regards them both as 'successful'. His objective for them is 'good relationship with partner and good health'. For Mrs Fraser he also adds, 'daytime activity'. Mr and Mrs Fraser are very fond of their social worker and they think highly of him. They are pleased that they have his home telephone number:

'. . . if there's any problems he knows I can get in touch with him and he's got our number . . . and I've got his own number as well as the office number. Now if he's not in the office you see I try to get in touch with him mostly at night time, usually at about 8 o'clock. Well it depends what time he gets back you see. . . . I know I've got a good social worker. . . .'

Frank and Sid Dean

Frank and Sid Dean are brothers of 45 and 53 respectively. They had difficult early lives as their father left home when they were small and their mother was left in financial difficulties without support. When their mother died they came to the attention of services as a result of their multiple debts and neglected home. They were moved to a specialist hospital where they lived for over a decade and from there they moved to a series of bedsits. For the period prior to their removal to the area in which they now live, they were 'of no fixed abode'. They were only able to get seasonal work in seaside resorts and a longstanding drink problem of Sid Dean caused him to lose jobs frequently.

Sid Dean is described as having a 'moderate' mental handicap. He is a very shy and quietly spoken man and he relies a great deal on his brother for help. He has a heart condition and an ulcer. His home carer describes Sid Dean's appearance as 'always immaculate' and in surprising contrast to his brother Frank, 'Sid's always incredibly clean and well turned out'. Unlike his brother, Sid Dean is no longer seeking employment and is content to attend a local centre of further education on a part-time basis. Frank Dean said: *'We're both on the sick. We had jobs on leisure beaches. I'd like a job but you can't get one.'* At the centre of further education, the brothers are having lessons in cookery, woodwork, literacy and numeracy. They are pleased with the coffee table and pan stand they have made.

When they moved from the seaside resort, their former social worker described Frank and Sid Dean as 'loners and wanderers' and he anticipated that they would require 'only a minimum of support'. It transpired that this was not the case. It was a matter of some concern that when they moved into their maisonette they had a series of debts, and money difficulties have since been a focus of social work support. Support with the management of their household and with hygiene is also given. Frank Dean regards the help they receive as inadequate: '*We get nowt. No help at all.*'

The brothers live in an inner city multi-storey estate of council housing. Their maisonette is sparsely furnished and is in a poor state of repair. It is close to boarded-up flats and is defaced with graffiti. They keep their curtains closed permanently to discourage intimidation from children. They have no contact with their neighbours:

'*It's not too bad . . . we've lived in worse. This is the best one we've had. Even though it's cold and there's a draught by the window. It's somewhere to go. . . . We was over there [in the same neighbourhood] for three years and that was terrible. There were kids all the way across the landing there, bashing the door in and everything. It's not so bad 'round here. We've had no kids here have we?*'

The brothers' social worker is concerned that her clients are lonely and that the cleanliness of their home is poor. Some time ago Frank Dean wrote to her and explained, '*I wont to meat odhoder pepol lick myself.*' Although they are anxious to participate in social activities during the day, the brothers did not like their local ATC and left after a few months. Frank Dean sees himself as having '*struggled on*' through their fourteen years of independent living.

Their limited incomes and difficulties with budgeting mean that they cannot afford to use the local launderette (they have no washing machine) and they cannot go into cafés for snacks or drinks. They mostly watch the TV in the evenings. At regular intervals the brothers call upon their social worker for a WRVS (Womens Royal Voluntary Service) note for free clothing. Their social worker describes them as 'moderately successful' and identifies 'social isolation' as their most significant problem. She cites as her objective for them: 'Self management in the community and help with clothing from the WRVS and a grant for shoes from a voluntary agency.'

Mr Thomas Conner

Mr Thomas Conner is very slightly built. He has a receding hairline and wears glasses. He is 52 years old and lives with his elderly and physically handicapped father, George Conner. The family originated from the south and for many years George Conner owned a family business. It was a large, general goods shop and Thomas Conner worked in this as a window dresser. When George Conner's wife died, his own health deteriorated and he had a stroke. Acknowledging that his son Thomas was unable to run the business alone, it was sold and father and son left the area. During their subsequent residence in a jointly purchased home, George Conner's health continued to deteriorate:

'I gave up my job to look after my father. I worked with me father then I worked as a kitchen porter. . . . I used to work at hotel, £25 a week I used to get. Stopped to look after dad. I do full time housework here now. I do decorating, I do the lot.'

George Conner's other son Wilf persuaded his father and brother to sell up and live with his family. In retrospect they regard this as an unwise move and Thomas Conner spoke with bitterness about this time in their lives:

'My brother got us to go and live with him. I stayed there to sell the house up. Dad came up here and he didn't like it so he phoned up one Saturday afternoon. Well I couldn't do nothing so it took me a while to sort it out. I got up there and he was black and blue from top to bottom. I said me brother, 'You been hitting me dad?' He said 'No, you're a fool.' Got no proof. Lots of rows, he hit me. I said, 'Look, just pack it up, leave me father alone.' He nearly put me eye out. . . . We had a lot of rows me and me brother. I used to be on the dole when I lived with him, £27 a week. He took the lot, the whole lot. I had nothing. . . . We went for a day out . . . the bus broke down and we had to wait for the next bus. We didn't get in 'till half past eleven at night. . . . There were two cars in the drive and dad couldn't get in with his zimmer. I asked my brother to move his car and he said, 'It's my drive, I'll do what I want to do.' He started a row . . . dad fell, he said 'Good, good, has he broke his neck?' I said 'Are you going to help us?' He said 'No.' Wilf doesn't give a damn. . . .'

George and Thomas Conner now live in their own home and no longer have any contact with Wilf Conner. They have been in their home for four years and Thomas Conner has full control of the running of the household. George Conner explained:

'We're away from them now. And now we're perfectly happy as we are. We're forgetting the past. Start a new life, I'm not very healthy to start it, but I'd like you to see the rest of the house. When we came in it was in a terrible state, Thomas has done it all. He's modernised everything . . . he does the cooking and everything . . . He has to dress me, undress me and wash me . . . he has to put dressings on me every night and morning . . . he takes me out too, shopping . . . . Relations arrived unexpectedly once, Thomas cooked a beautiful meal, he did all that and they left quite happy. . . .'

Their home is very attractive and a justifiable source of pride. Thomas Conner described the work he has done to their house and his daily activities:

'We had a burst pipe before dad come out of hospital. I got people in to do it. Then they said it would be OK. It was like a river in here, all flooded. He should have been coming home. I asked them to hold him back. . . . I sleep with him. We

sleep together. See if I was in another room I couldn't never hear him . . . I get me father up. He stops in bed in the morning, 'till about 11 o'clock, that gives me time to get the cleaning up done, get dinner and all those things. 'Cept on Wednesdays, I go to Steve across the road, a friend of mine. We're all friends around here. He helps me [in the vegetable garden] and I help him do his garden. Gives me something to do, gets me out. I've got a moped too. I get out a bit on that driving out. . . . Dad wants a ring [to sit on]. He sits there [in a wheel chair] all day and he gets sores. He wants something like a cushion. If you're sitting there eight hours it's uncomfy. . . . I want to get him one of those chairs. Something high up like a rubber ring so you get air. . . . I get me money once a fortnight, dole money, £40. I get £1.05p to look after me father, attendance. It's not much is it? Don't even get food. It's a disgrace. I'm sick because me back keeps going. Put meself out lifting. I have to hold on tight to him or I drop him. Sometimes I put him back on the bed or chair again if me back starts to give me a twitch. . . . I made dad a birthday cake, we had a birthday party here. This is the advert [notice] I put in [the paper] for him. I thought I would do it and I have done it. . . .'

Thomas Conner's social worker acknowledges that her client is very able and inevitably, she regards him as 'successful'. With reference to specific help, she assists her client in liaising with the DHSS, and counsels in respect of interpersonal issues. She is concerned about Thomas Conner's social life and leisure activities, a concern shared by her client:

'We've got some friends around us, neighbours that's all. Social worker comes once a month and sees that we're all right, that we're OK. If I got any queries I just go round the corner [to the social services] and sort it out. . . . People from the Mission Hall come at weekends. One of them helps me with the shopping. If I walk down it's easier for the two of us. You carry these great big bags. I've got to rush round, get it done quick and run back and see he's all right. If I've forgot three things I've to go. I had to take my moped for its MOT, it passed it. . . . We need someone else to come down and see dad. We get fed up here sitting on our own. He needs a change, a break. . . .'

Thomas Conner is concerned that he cannot read or write. His father explained that his son had lost his education during the war and was 'backward' as a result of an explosion. Thomas Conner said that if anyone asked him to read he said he had, *'left his reading glasses at home'*. This is unsatisfactory to him, however, and placing his hand on his chest he said, *'I know I'm lying in here'*.

'I must say I can't read or write. It worries me more. One time I used to be able to write. I got someone coming in to teach me. He used to be a head teacher, he had to give it up, his health bad. . . . I go to night school down the square, I used to go there. Now he comes here twice a week. Wednesdays and Fridays I'm learning about the Bible. . . .'

Miss Gina Shaw

Miss Shaw is 64 years old. The oldest of seven children, she lived with her family until she was fourteen. Her mother died when she was twelve and an aunt moved into the family home to assist with the young children. Miss Shaw's father was often out of work. Described as having a 'severe' mental handicap, it is believed that Miss Shaw's initial diagnosis of being 'feebleminded' resulted from brain damage following a fall.

Although Miss Shaw was keen to help in the family home, her father was anxious for her to be cared for. It was believed that Miss Shaw was in moral danger and consequently she was placed in a specialist hospital. During her 25 years of residence in hospital Miss Shaw had limited contact with her family. She was described as 'childish in her manner and unable to read or write'. It was thought, however, that Miss Shaw could manage in a supervised setting outside the hospital. Contact with her family indicated that they were unable to offer accommodation and her father's whereabouts were unknown.

Before Miss Shaw was transferred 'on licence' from hospital, a position was found for her as a domestic in a private school. She shared a room with two other domestics and worked mostly in the kitchen. The headmistress's review of Miss Shaw's work was initially negative: 'Gina has no idea at all of housework, or indeed anything apart from peeling potatoes. I really don't want to take her back because she's so pathetically keen to do well.' Regardless of this, Miss Shaw continued at the school and claimed to enjoy working there. She was persistently afraid that she would have to return to hospital. Mrs Craig, the headmistress, offered to become Miss Shaw's guardian and this offer was accepted. Twelve months after her removal to the school, a progress report noted the following:

> 'Gina is generally well behaved and a good worker. She can be relied upon to do local errands. She is however easily led and is somewhat put upon by the other girls who have her running their personal errands. She is the only one who can be allowed out on her own. . . . She has a good memory and can remember a few simple items for shopping. She can be trusted with money but has no sense of value.'

During her residence in the school Miss Shaw enjoyed doing jigsaws, embroidery and watching television. She visited other women 'on licence' from the hospital at the Salvation Army home. Miss Shaw has no fond memories of her residence in the school:

> *'I were in an institution, it were a convent. I came out of institution and went into service with Mrs Craig. It was a boarding school and I didn't like it. No, it was all right in the servant's hall, but she used to get nasty. One day she came, I were doing me bedroom out and she came one Sunday to me and said 'Are you going out?' So I said, 'Yes, I'm going to.' You see I had a stepmother and I was going to*

her house for tea. She wouldn't let me and she smacked me face. Yes, she was
terrible to me. So me sister got me away from there and I was down at the hostel in
town, then I went to another hostel, then I went to live near here, then here. . . .'

Mrs Craig's guardianship lasted for five years and was allowed to lapse. After
eleven years, the school was sold and Miss Shaw was transferred to a hostel. She
had friends living in the hostel and she was already a member of the social club. On
admission to the hostel Miss Shaw was described as 'a pathetic drudge, shabby,
looking old and wearing terrible clothes. She's settled down and is happy . . . ideal
for a group home.' Miss Shaw lived in the hostel for nine years and during this
period she met and became engaged to Brian. Plans were made for the two of them
to move into their own home:

'I used to see me boyfriend . . . a shame wasn't it? He died in his sleep. We got
engaged to get married an' all. I've had the ring on this finger since he put it on. I
haven't taken it off. We would have been in a flat. . . . Sheila [social worker]
would have got us a flat 'cos he was on about it . . . I would have been with Brian
and we would have married and settled down now. . . .'

Currently Miss Shaw lives in a homely and attractive three-bedroomed house
with two friends, Miss Maura Conway and Miss Vera Carroll, both of whom are in
their 60s. Miss Carroll's health is poor and Miss Shaw and Miss Conway do the
bulk of the household duties. Although there are occasional conflicts in the house,
in the main they get on and they are supportive of each other:

'We clean up every morning when we get up . . . Vera doesn't do anything at the
moment 'cos she's not well . . . we send washing to the laundry, a gentleman
comes on Monday and brings it back on Thursday. . . . Mr Johnson [social
worker] and Sheila come here. We like them and a friend Veronica. She said she's
going to take us for a picnic in the summer didn't she Maura? We've got a next
door neighbour, Judy and Sam. They've got a dog and a cat like our cat, they're
very, very nice. Anything we want they'll come, won't they? I baked a cake for Mr
Johnson's children and iced it . . . he came and had his tea and he said, 'Do you
want this for your tea?' he said. Well she thought it were real and it went up like a
jack-in-the-box! He's a tormentor Mr Johnson and he says to me, 'Come on now
Gina, have your tea, it'll be cold.' But it was a salad! And we went to his house for
tea. . . .'

Miss Shaw's sister emigrated to Australia several years ago and they regularly
write to each other. Miss Shaw saved for a holiday and in 1981 she spent six weeks
with her. Miss Shaw enjoyed the visit enormously and with the guidance of her
social worker, is currently saving for another trip:

'We went to see a gold mine . . . we had a picnic in the park and they have a
barbecue, you take your own stove and do a barbecue. . . . Me sister's daughter

lives up in the mountains and it was lovely. We went Christmas eve and they had carols in candlelight. . . . She took me to the pictures and I thought we had to get out the car, and she said 'No, stop in the car and you look at them.' You had a thing to put in your ear. . . . I saw Max Bygraves, then I went to the Tattoo. . . . I helped me sister to decorate the Christmas tree up and they make their own chocolate. . . . I've got three brothers in Australia and one near here. He doesn't bother with me. . . .'

Miss Shaw enjoys frequent contact with her social worker who visits the house more than once a week. Although he is concerned that his client cannot handle medical problems, he regards her as 'successful' and his main objective for her is 'good health and good relationships with co-residents'.

Mr William Clark

Mr Clark is 36 years old and is described as having a 'mild' mental handicap. Little is known of his early life. One of three children, when his mother died he lived briefly with his siblings. This did not work out and he was transferred to a hostel. Then for unknown reasons he moved to another hostel, and for the last five years he has been living independently. Initially this was in a group home for six people and currently he lives with two friends, Miss Karen Walsh and Miss Jessica Barnes. When I met Mr Clark and his co-residents they were sitting, watching TV and each was covered with a sleeping bag. I was invited to share one as well. Mr Clark explained that they were *'saving on heating'*.

'I've been here for about a year. . . . I lived in Grantham Street before, I used to live there. It was very nice but I didn't get on with the other fella. He was moaning all the time . . . This is the best place. . . . The Director of Social Services is next door. He's only there temporary 'till he gets his house done up. Seems very nice. When they went there the house was empty. We just know one man in all the bungalows. . . .'

Mr Clark's appearance is very striking. He is a tall and handsome man who wears smart clothes, shaded glasses and earrings. He smiles often and easily. Mr Clark enjoys his current home, the company of his friends, Karen and Jessica, and the housework:

'I cook all sorts, don't I Jessica? All sorts of meals . . . we do it at night time. . . . We have a washing machine but it's out of order at the moment. It leaks . . . we wash over the weekends usually. . . . In the evenings we just relax and watch TV, don't we Karen, don't we? If there's a good film on we watches that. Coronation Street or Brookside. . . . Karen and I will have a go at the decorating. . . .'

Miss Walsh outlined how important Mr Clark is in the house: '*I do most of the cooking, but William is the chef.*' Visibly pleased, Mr Clark responded '*I'm quite flattered over that, quite enthusiastic you know.*' Mr Clark and his friends live in a modern and spacious bungalow next door to an old people's home. It is attractive and they take pride in it. They are buying household items gradually: '*We bought a freezer. Karen's mum put the cash down for it and we pay her back, £5 a week each . . . Alex [social worker] does the finances. . . .*'

Mr Clark has been working throughout his residence in the bungalow and his social worker rates him as 'doing exceptionally well'.

'*Well I'm out at work all day. I work voluntary in an old people's home. Very nice, I like it don't I Jessica? Very nice, my boss is a woman, a lady, female you know. She's very nice. We just actually asked if there was any vacancies and she said 'Yes, I've got one if you want to come in.' I'm looking after old people, care assistant work, very nice, very good actually. I take the men to the toilet.*'

Mr Clark's social worker sees his client weekly and he specifically encourages leisure activities. He has two concerns: Mr Clark is 'inclined to chat to children' (and does not appreciate that he is often being teased); and on odd occasions, 'he may need correcting in matters of complete honesty'. In spite of these concerns, the social worker is delighted with his client's progress and he hopes that Mr Clark may 'continue living in the community like any other person'.

Mr Michael Hickey

Mr Hickey is 43 years old. He is a solidly built man who walks with a pronounced limp. This is his only visible disability. He is a very reflective person and thinks carefully before he speaks. His speech is slow and deliberate.

The four young Hickeys had an unsettled childhood. Their father left home and when their mother died they all went into a children's home. During their residential careers they were separated and Mr Hickey was in six children's homes in total before finally being transferred to a specialist hospital:

'*When I was sixteen the home was closing down. They didn't have enough boys and girls to keep us there. They were put in another home and I was put in hospital for fifteen years. . . . I moved a lot like I said before, you've got to help yourself in this world Margaret, you don't just sit around and wait for somebody to help you. You've got to get on your two feet and you've got to try to help yourself. . . . I came to the hostel and stayed there for six years. Then I moved to the housing unit. It was all right. I moved from that place to here. Luckily the Officer in Charge [of the hostel] she got me in here to see if I could look after myself, which I can, and the Friends of the Hostel furnished it.*'

During the early part of Mr Hickey's residence in hospital, he was not an ideal resident. He was described as 'quick-tempered and aggressive'. He did not like mixing with other people. Currently, Mr Hickey's social worker sees his client infrequently, pointing out that he needs 'support and guidance of a very general nature'. He has a full-time job and he is equal to managing his finances. He enjoys his friends and leisure, he plans and pays for his holidays each year, and he has many interests:

'It's a great job. I'm a cleaner. Next Monday I've been ten years and one week on the same job and there have been no complaints about me. I have not been cautioned, I have not been warned and my record is clean. . . . I do the shopping on a Friday afternoon. . . . I come in from work, the washing I put in the machine. I go down to the Post Office and pay me rent and I go to the Abbey National [Building Society] and put money in. Then I go to the Asda and do me shopping. I come back and take the washing out of the machine, spin dry it, into the basket, into the cupboard. I iron the washing when I come back from work on a Saturday afternoon, you got to keep it clean. I work to a system like I just said. My girlfriend comes at weekends. . . . I breed birds, go fishing and I've got country and western records. . . . There's a pub I go in on Thursday nights and there's country and western in there. The ladies go dressed in skirts, guns, the lot and the men go in cowboy gear. Two of the singers do a lot of charity work for the handicapped, they have shooters and ropes. I can't remember them all there's so many. . . . I don't sit here all night unless there's something really good on television, like nature ones, a good cowboy or a good murder. . . . I can't keep still. I like people to come here.'

Mr Hickey lives in a small and comfortable bungalow on a modern, warden-controlled housing unit. There are communal facilities, but each bungalow is self-contained. Mr Hickey knows many of his neighbours even though he describes himself as the sort who keeps himself to himself. He appreciates the benefits of warden controlled housing:

'If they talk to me, I talk to them. If I wanted the warden, there's what you call a speaker on the wall there . . . that's what we want, disabled. You just pull that, but I don't need it . . . one time I called, my back locked. I was kneeling down and I got a pain.'

Mr Hickey's social worker regards his client as 'successful' and his objective for his client is 'to try to ensure that he can maintain himself in the community. Michael is a very capable person and this shouldn't be too difficult'. I asked Mr Hickey what advice he would give to somebody who was about to move into their own home from a hospital or hostel:

'It depends on what background they come from. If they're in a hostel, they'd have to move very slowly. I mean they couldn't jump right out of a hostel into a

*home by yourself. . . . If I need any help I go across to the hostel and Mrs Wilkin
and staff, they help me. If I need a button or something, they do the thread in the
needle, see my fingers are bent. But if they're moving out, there's one thing
they've got to get used to very quick, that's the loneliness. If men and women
come out of the hostel they've got to be able to cook, look after themselves, keep
themselves clean, the bungalow house or flat clean. I mean when I first come here
Mrs Wilkin used to teach me how to cook. Now I know how to cook. If you need
any help like sewing, the letter I don't understand, you just take them across to the
hostel, and they explain them to you.'*

SUMMARY

These accounts of nine people's lives necessarily leave a lot unsaid. They demonstrate the considerable achievements of these people, the diversity of the difficulties they experience and the variety of their lifestyles and circumstances. The
individuality of these people's lives should be borne in mind while reading the
following chapters. Two themes merit mention as these shed some light on the
difficulties of independent living.

Money

The first is people's need for assistance with money management. It is a major
preoccupation of social workers, as few people are able to budget without assistance (Flynn, 1986c). The majority of people are in receipt of supplementary
benefits and the complexity of this fragmented income means that most need help
both in liaising with the DHSS, in completing DHSS forms and paying bills – for
example, Mr and Mrs Fraser, Miss Shaw and Mr Clark. The issue is more complex
for those who cannot read. A number of people talked about showing their letters
to others.

Another facet of money management concerns income. The range of incomes
for the people described in this chapter is from £20 to £60 a week. Given that people
with mental handicap may experience problems with abstract thinking, it is to be
expected that budgeting difficulties will result for many people. This is especially
the case when incomes are so limited. People living in groups such as Miss Shaw
and Mr Clark are financially better off as they are able to pool their resources. So,
Miss Shaw has financed a trip to Australia and Mr Clark and his co-residents have
purchased a freezer with financial help. The experiences of Frank and Sid Dean
and Mr Carney are typical. Their debts are being paid weekly resulting in the
regular erosion of their money, often imposing impossible restrictions on their
lives.

Social isolation

A second theme that emerges is that of social isolation to the extent that social workers are almost inevitably regarded as friends. Miss Mason is desperate to be friends with people and is depressed that her overtures to her neighbours are shunned. Mr Carney visits his social worker daily and he asked me if I would marry him. Mr Payne has no friends outside college. The issue is just as pressing for people who have partners or live with friends. Frank and Sid Dean live in abject poverty and are lonely. This situation is barely relieved by part-time attendance at a centre for further education. They do not regard themselves as assisted by social services personnel. Mrs Fraser and Thomas Conner experience loneliness and Mr Hickey says that this is something that people '*have to get used to very quick*'.

The other facet of social isolation concerns people's interpersonal skills and difficulties. Reasons for the failure of people with mental handicap to acquire social and interpersonal skills have been suggested by research into their learning difficulties. Some aspects of the latter are short attention spans, the reduced ability to transfer learning, slow reaction times, inability to anticipate consequences and difficulties selecting the most relevant cues and dimensions. Social interactions are often highly verbal in nature and yet people with mental handicap frequently experience difficulty in processing and retaining complex verbal information. All of these factors have implications for the acquisition of interpersonal skills which are by nature complex (Argyle, 1969). Thus Miss Mason's home carer counsels her about contact with her neighbours and friends; Mr Carney's tendency to violence means that he is not eligible for day services; and Mr and Mrs Fraser, and Miss Shaw and friends are all known to experience interpersonal difficulties. For Mr Carney and Miss Mason in particular, this results in loneliness.

The lives and concerns of these people often parallel those of their non mentally handicapped neighbours in that they face the necessary repetitions of household tasks; shopping; budgeting; travelling; dealing with people; dealing with correspondence; sometimes wishing for employment and more adequate incomes; and sometimes, decent housing. It should be recalled however, that almost all of these people have spent long periods of their lives in isolated, specialist communities; that they need assistance from social services and CMHT personnel to greater and lesser degrees to manage their lives; and that they all live with the label of 'mental handicap'.

Finally, it should be noted that this chapter does not present a static picture of people's lives. Even at the time of writing, changes are in the air for some people. People's living arrangements change over time and the reasons for change include in isolation or combination: the poor repair of a tenancy; hostility from a neighbourhood; interpersonal difficulties in a tenancy; and/or preference to live elsewhere/with somebody else.

4
The People, Their Daily Activities and Backgrounds

This study is predictive and from the outset was committed to gathering quantitative information. While there are pockets of quantitative information about specific topics, I am uncertain that this accurately reflects what people are like. Thus the preceding chapter is an effort to portray nine people's lives in a way that information regarding frequencies, for example, totally obscures.

In this chapter, background information about the 88 people is presented. It begins with an account of my approach and general impressions of the people I met and turns to consider aspects of people's presentation, the things we notice about people when we first meet them: their ages; their gender; how they look, including any speech and medical problems they have. It then moves on to a consideration of what they do: their skills and the things they have difficulty with; and the way they pass their time. Finally, the little that is known of their background, their classification, the way they see themselves and their views about specialist residential facilities are presented.

THE INTERVIEWS

Prior to the onset of the main study I regarded the interview schedule as one piece in the jigsaw of four measures. My views about this changed over the three years and now I regard the interviews as one of the most enlightening and informative parts of the study. When I began to visit people I was ill-prepared for my reception as a guest, the warmth with which I was received into people's homes and the many overtures to friendship I was offered. Initially I was startled by the readiness and frankness with which people talked to me. I expected to have to work at establishing that uncertain state of 'rapport' (Oakley, 1981). I have no doubt that a structured interview schedule would not have had this effect. Simply having a list of topics I hoped we could address during the interview enabled people to talk at length, or not, as they wished. For a small number of people the interviews were reciprocal and I was asked questions about my life, activities and preferences.

In the tradition established by Finch (1984), James (1984), Jenkins (1984) and Eastwood (1987), I believe that it is helpful to relate my impressions of the interviews over the course of the study. On many occasions, when I arrived at a person's house, I was regarded as an extra pair of hands to assist with whatever task was preoccupying, such as setting an alarm clock, reading/explaining the contents of a letter, replacing a light bulb, helping to complete a form, putting up curtains, or writing a letter. So the length of the interviews varied according to people's desire to talk about themselves and their lives and the tasks for which my assistance was sought.

Almost half of the interviews took place in the evening, and I found that if supper was customary in a particular household then a place had been set for me. I do not recall any interviews when I was not offered tea or coffee. In one household, prior to my arrival, two women prepared sandwiches for my return car journey to Manchester which they estimated would be long. Some people regarded me as an extension of services, irrespective of their social worker's explanation, my introductory letter and explanation at the beginning of interviews. At the end of one interview a woman living with her female friend asked, '*What do you do? She thinks you research our minds. I thought you was testing people.*' After this, my work and the study were described in more detail and I invited people to ask me about these.

It became clear that my assertion that I would only be visiting people on one occasion was either unheard or unattended. A number of people described painful experiences of isolation, followed by requests that I should continue to visit them. One woman rang me after she had been mugged and requested my assistance with transferring to another area. In total, these events tie in with the impression of social isolation reported in Chapter 3. People wanted friends and any interested stranger was a candidate.

I was concerned about the potential of the interviews to exploit people and by the unquestioning frankness of some. When I asked one woman about her income, she opened a drawer containing her pension book and cash and remarked that they were '*in a secret place*'. It came as no surprise that many social workers keep a check on their clients' finances in order to ensure that they have not willingly hosted hawkers of insurance/encyclopaedias/mail order goods, etc.

In the following sections, the more quantitative features of people's lives are described. As in the succeeding chapters, extensive use is made of material from the interviews.

AGE AND GENDER

The age range of the 50 men and 38 women I met is from 22 to 79 years with an average of 47 years (SD: 13.4). The age of one woman was not known. So there is a wide spread of ages with a concentration of people (38) over the age of 50.

APPEARANCE

This is an area that until recently has not been explored in relation to people with mental handicap. Social psychological research has demonstrated that attractive people are perceived and treated more favourably than less attractive people (Adams, 1977; Berscheid and Walster, 1974). Invariably our appearance has consequences for the way in which others react towards us (Rumsey, Bull and Gahagan, 1982). Some people with mental handicap do look different. Miller and Gwynne (1972) have described the process that being conspicuous creates:

> If I have a visible handicap, your behaviour towards me will be different in gross or subtle ways from your behaviour towards able-bodied associates; accordingly, my response to you is different from theirs to you; your image of me as different is confirmed; my image of myself is affected by your image of me; thus, I am in reality different. (p. 72)

A number of studies have supported the importance of people's appearance and good grooming in community living (Moen, Bogen and Aanes 1975; Gollay *et al.*, 1978). Richardson, Koller and Katz (1985) developed a measure of atypical appearance and tested it on 165 young adults with mild mental handicap. They found that these people were atypical in their appearance when compared to their non mentally handicapped peers. The appearance measure developed by Richardson and colleagues is extensive and was considered inappropriate for use in this study. Consequently a briefer measure was used, noting the presence/absence of atypicalities within the dimensions of size, facial appearance, bodily appearance, body movement and clothes. I completed the measure after each interview. I wished to explore the consequences of conspicuousness for people who are living independently. While people spontaneously talked about many aspects of their lives, it is noteworthy that very few people made any reference to their appearance:

> *'I'm getting fat . . . I had hysterectomy done. . . . So you see I put weight on. . . . How old do you think I am? I feel 98. I'm getting fat.'*

> *'Me brother had a good head of hair I do know that. Thicker than thick it were. . . . I'm not bald, it's me high forehead that . . . just how it grows like that.'*

> *'I'm supposed to be on a diet . . . I try to look after meself. They keep telling me to lose weight but what do I do? Carry on eating . . . once I was so heavy I broke me caliper. . . . Listen, I do not wear that thing [caliper] in the house. It annoys me. I could throw it through the window.'*

> *'See I've got a lot of scars. That's from where my father used to beat me. And if you look at this eye, you can see it's different. I was pushed when I was a child and I can hardly see out of that eye.'*

'I just like chips you see. Trouble is it makes me fat and I can't get into me clothes properly and he [brother] gets upset about that. I take after me mum. She was big you see. She had trouble with her clothes.'

My ratings of people's appearance are presented in Table 4.1. Only one person in the study population is conspicuous as a consequence of Down's syndrome. It will be seen that it is both static (for example, weight and gait) and dynamic features (clothes) which make some people more noticeable than others. (See Flynn 1985a for information regarding interrater reliability.)

Table 4.1 *People's conspicuousness*

Distinguishing features	Present	Absent	Distinguishing features	Present	Absent
Very tall	8	69	Physical handicaps	8	80
Very small	11		Unusual posture	11	77
Very large	17	64	Unusual gait	14	74
Very thin	7		Rocking	3	85
Unusual features	8	80	Odd mannerisms	3	85
Facial asymmetry	3	85	Clothes bizarre	1	87
Facial twitches	7	81	Clothes inappropriate	5	83
Use of prosthesis	6	82	Clothes poorly cared for	14	74

Some 57 people in total have at least one of the features listed in Table 4.1, 38 people have two or more features that make them conspicuous and fifteen people have three or more of these features. It will be seen in Chapter 8 that the more conspicuous a person is, that is, having a multiplicity of conspicuous attributes, the greater the likelihood of social aversion and victimisation. Thus appearance is a dimension which cannot be ignored by services involved in the placement of people with mental handicap in their own homes.

SPEECH AND MEDICAL CONDITIONS

People's speech and medical conditions are presented in Table 4.2. It may have been noted in Chapter 3 that information regarding people's background is somewhat scant and the same is true of their medical conditions. The problems listed in Table 4.2 were noted in case records, in other words they had come to the attention of social workers as a result of appointments to be made and/or assistance given in managing medication. Social workers were asked to note the severity of the conditions listed. Given that social workers checked/amended this information without any guidelines, it should be pointed out that Table 4.2 only crudely suggests the speech and medical conditions of people. No attempt was made to validate this information from medical records.

Table 4.2 *Speech and medical condition*

Problems	None	Mild	Severe
Visual	59	26	3
Mobility	72	15	1
Speech impairment	69	11	8
Epilepsy	75	10	3
Hearing	81	6	1
Heart	82	6	–
Mental illness	81	5	2
Metabolic	83	4	1
Respiratory	84	4	–
Gastrointestinal	85	1	2

There are difficulties in defining each of the conditions itemised, and in respect of epilepsy, for example, this is outlined by Richardson *et al.* (1980). In respect of speech, it will be seen that eight people have severe difficulties and a further eleven experience mild problems. My views of people's ability to speak during the interviews concurred with the case records. Mild visual problems affect some 26 people and a further three have severe difficulties with their sight. Of these, two people attend specialist facilities for people who are blind. Sixteen people have problems with mobility, but taking into account the age range of the people I met this is perhaps not surprising.

Additional medically oriented issues were gathered from the case records. It appears that eight people have periods of heavy drinking; eight are heavy smokers; 20 have 'a weight problem'; twelve do not follow prescribed medical treatment; and thirteen people are subject to depression and their 'general deterioration' has been observed. While this information does indicate that the activities of some people are curtailed by their mental state and habits, these figures are limited because of missing information.

It should be pointed out that the severity of the medical problems of some people impinge on their lives to an arguably greater extent than mental handicap alone. For example, for one woman the blind centre she attends is an important feature of her social life. She associates largely with people with visual handicap.

I was interested to note that one man made strategic use of his spasticity and communication difficulties. He frequently visits friends in the far north but only purchases a ticket for a short journey. When quizzed at his destination he feigns deafness and pretends that he has no speech.

SKILLS

In recent years, procedures to teach a variety of community living skills to people with mental handicap have been developed. Most of the people in this study who resided in hospitals and hostels have been trained in these skills, although nothing is known about the quality of this preparation. Typically though, hospitals, hostels and adult training centres (ATCs) are not ideal training locations with their centralised services, physical and staffing constraints. Only latterly have 'training flats' developed, allowing people to practise self-help and home care skills in settings which closely approximate those of ordinary flats and houses.

Table 4.3 *People's skills*

Skill	Can do	Can do with help	Cannot do	Do not know	Problem*
Housekeeping	59	26	3	–	5
Dressing appropriately	80	8	–	–	2
Managing finances	31	47	10	–	5
Making everyday decisions	49	37	2	–	3
Handling relationship with man/woman friend	47	31	3	7	7
Handling interpersonal relationships	40	40	3	5	6
Managing time and planning activities in advance	45	39	3	1	–
Paying bills	30	43	15	–	5
Handling medical problems	35	49	4	–	6
Cooking own meals	65	18	4	1	1
Handling shopping	63	24	1	–	2
Using public transport	84	2	1	1	–
Maintaining standards of personal hygiene	62	23	3	–	5
Doing laundry	60	22	5	1	3
Maintaining proper sleep habits	80	4	1	3	–

Can do indicates that the person is functioning effectively in the use of this skill; these activities are performed at a reasonable level of competence.

Can do with help indicates fair or marginal competence; these activities are not routine and the person needs prompts and/or assistance.

Cannot do indicates inability of the person to manage in spite of efforts to do so; assistance is routinely required for these activities.

Do not know indicates absence of information concerning the person's skills.

* Skill is a particular problem to the social worker

The skills itemised in Table 4.3 were assessed by people's social workers and were selected from published materials associated with independent living (for example, Clark, Kivitz and Rosen, 1968; Hill and Bruininks, 1977; Bruininks *et al.*, 1981). The listing is deliberately brief. It was determined with social services personnel that a detailed assessment schedule would be beyond the obvious knowledge of social workers. Assessment schedules did not feature in people's case records. From Table 4.3 it is clear that in terms of using public transport, dressing appropriately and maintaining proper sleep habits, people are largely accomplished. The skills for which assistance is particularly required are managing finances, paying bills and handling medical problems. Although there were no cross-checks for the reliability of this information, in general it appears that living independently is not solely for the most competent in independent living training programmes. Some people require a great deal of assistance to enable them to live in their own homes and yet continue to do so. It will be seen that social services departments, co-residents and families augment people's competence to ameliorate the effects of their learning problems.

It should be noted that during the interviews, over three-quarters of the people I met described their routines regarding money management, cooking, laundry, shopping and cleaning. The following quotations elaborate on this and also give some indication of the variety of help people receive.

'If I get bills I write a cheque and the bank here [at work] sorts things out.'

'I give my home carer electric, rent, things I have to pay out.'

'I got mates down the road and they make me tea. I do me own lunch at weekends.'

'We do it [cook] in turns.'

'I do all my own washing here. I have a machine what my grandma gave me . . . the bedding and curtains I take to the launderette 'cos I can't do big things. I go to the launderette now and then like, but it's that dear it's terrible.'

'I made sure I got a washer [machine] dearie. I'm not trailing down there. I said, "I want a washing machine." I do it when I get a pile.'

'She [sister] likes going round the shops so we go a lot on Saturdays. We go to Manchester a lot and buy the things we need from there.'

'We do a lot of washing but I think it's not necessary really.'

'I buy bacon, eggs and butter. . . . It takes a hard job for her [home carer] to find me because sometimes I hide away from her. I like playing little games' [such as teasing the home carer].

'I do it [cleaning] when it's dirty. Sheila [social worker] helps me.'

'I sort it out [cleaning] myself, mostly at weekends.'

Social workers were asked to specify what concerns they had regarding their clients' skills. These were itemised on behalf of 26 people and a representative selection is presented below. The listing suggests that people's social workers see a wide range of problems affecting their client's lives. Many of their concerns refer to practical skill deficits which should be relatively easy to remedy. However, there are other concerns which relate to more abstract, interpersonal skills which are not easy to either explain or to teach, such as vulnerability to exploitation.

- She is easily influenced by others.
- Only concern is that he could not function without the existing (daily) level of help.
- Always values people's advice and therefore restricts her decision making and competence.
- She has never managed to achieve a satisfactory relationship with a man. She likes men and I feel she may benefit from the right sort of relationship.
- He is impatient to get a 'proper' job with unrealistic expectations given the unemployment situation.
- Cleanliness is not good.
- Will sister always be there to look after him?
- Vulnerability in relation to his friendships.
- Personal clothing often dirty and worn.
- Concern regarding the lack of non-vocational classes available. There are few appropriate day classes.
- Problems with vandals and youngsters who get money from client.
- She is basically idle and also vulnerable concerning giving money to her married sister.

DAILY ACTIVITIES

People's work/day activities (of the 9am to 5pm variety) are presented in Table 4.4. It will be seen from the table that the 88 people can be divided into two groups. The first includes those who are unemployed or retired and their lives may be loosely described as 'unstructured'. This group accommodates half of the people I met. The second group includes people who are self-supporting through competitive and sheltered employment, those who attend colleges, ATCs, those who engage in voluntary work, and those three who are actively seeking work. In contrast to the former group, these people's lives may be described as 'structured'. Most people receive DHSS benefits, or baseline income which may be supplemented by additional earnings of no more than £4.00.

The fourteen people who expressed pleasure and satisfaction regarding their daily activities were almost always those who have structured days. The seventeen people who expressed varying degrees of dissatisfaction were consistently those who have unstructured days. Eleven unemployed people professed a desire for an 'ordinary' job. (The tapes of the interviews, transcriptions and field notes were all used to rate people's satisfaction, from, 0 = positive comment(s), observation(s) to 4 = negative comment(s), observation(s). If people expressed a desire to change their circumstances, for example if they said they wanted a job, this was noted as it indicates dissatisfaction; see Flynn (1986b) and Flynn and Saleem (1986) for further details.

Table 4.4 *People's daily activities*

Work/day activity		Number of people engaged in these
Unemployed, not seeking work	} unstructured	{ 24
Retired		20
Adult Training Centre		17
Open employment		12
College of Further Education	} structured	6
Sheltered employment		3
Unemployed, seeking work		3
Voluntary work		3

Activities outside the home can be an important source of social contacts, permitting association with a wide variety of people. These 88 people are poorly represented in the workforce. Boredom is a conspicuous problem for some people, most particularly for those who are unemployed. Their long-term unemployment status leaves them without hope of finding employment and frustrated by their inability to do so. It is important to note that for some people, unemployment is preferable to attending ATCs. Of the people who have opted to withdraw from ATCs, their criticisms of these concern the rules, insufficient remuneration, and dislike of association with people with mental handicap. The three people who are actively seeking work make at least weekly visits to their local job centres. Others have become despondent over time and cease to make such regular visits.

Work occupies a lot of time in our lives and it contributes to the way in which we see ourselves and the way we are seen by others. The influence of our work-life on our non-work-life is pervasive (see, for example, Kabanoff, 1980; Near, Rice and Hunt, 1980; Staines, 1980). Work is a way of satisfying personal needs ranging from the basic necessities to promoting higher order outlets for self-actualisation (Sullivan, 1972). Of the people in full-time employment there has been little fluctuation in their individual employment careers. They have all been employed for several years and they have excellent employment records. Their jobs include hospital portering, book binding, electrical maintenance, assembly line work and gardening.

The fact that work plays an important role in our lives explains the interest of researchers in the employment of people who have left hospitals and hostels. Kernan and Koegal (1980) suggest that there are three kinds of studies regarding people's work: follow-up studies that distinguish the 'successful' from the 'unsuccessful' populations; studies that attempt to suggest reasons for vocational success and failure; and studies concerning the success of specific vocational rehabilitation programmes (see Goldstein, 1964; Cobb, 1972; and Tizard, 1965, for reviews of the first two). Although the studies vary considerably in the way in which they were carried out, Kernan and Koegal (1980) observe: '. . . a consistent tendency does seem to emerge across the majority of these research efforts. Put simply, a high proportion of retarded adults do appear to make satisfactory vocational adjustments and eventually disappear into the general population' (p. 3).

Whelan and Speake (1981) summarised research findings concerning the areas that merit attention if people with mental handicap are to achieve satisfactory vocational adjustment. These include: sufficient preparation; work habits, skills and attitudes; job search skills; interpersonal skills; personality factors; general social competence; community skills; work-related academic skills; and self-help skills. The accomplishments of the 88 people in these areas are not known.

Unemployment is a social reality in Britain and a significant problem. There is a growing body of research showing that the effects of unemployment extend far beyond the immediate financial hardships (Johnson-Saylor, 1984). Unemployment affects health and mortality and depression is a frequently reported companion (Oliver and Pomicter, 1981). Gladstone (1985) has outlined the failure of a history of measures to facilitate the employment of disabled people in this country since the First World War:

> One of the effects of the economic recession of the 1980s is that disabled people who were regarded as 'essential manpower' forty years before are now increasingly seen as 'surplus labour'. Not only is the rate of unemployment for workers registered as disabled significantly higher than that for the population as a whole, there is also evidence which suggests that disabled people are disproportionately represented among the long term unemployed. (pp. 103–104)

This picture is corroborated by the Manpower Services Commission (1982). From their analysis they find that, '. . . once unemployed, disabled people are likely to experience much greater problems in regaining work than unemployed people generally.'

Some nine social workers indicated that they were involved in seeking employment for their clients, undaunted by the high number of unemployed people. In September 1983 there were over 3.1 million unemployed people, giving an unemployment rate of 13.3% (Central Statistical Office, 1983). Unemployment is unevenly spread across the country and North-West England is one of the worst affected regions.

The Central Statistical Office (1983) reports that the most frequent daily activities of people who are unemployed are housework, shopping and job-hunting (but the longer the period of unemployment, the less time is spent job-seeking). Younger age groups stay in bed until late and visit the town more frequently than their older counterparts. Sport is an important activity for people in their mid-20s to mid-30s, while older people get their exercise by walking. Some of the following quotations outline a range of people's views about their daily activities irrespective of their employment status. They mostly support the observation that people who have structured days are more satisfied with their 9am to 5pm lives. One man living with his partner said:

'I've finished now 'till Monday. Work for Water Board. It's all right. I've been there since I started and I'll be retiring this June 'cos my birthday's on a Sunday.'

A man living in a group home with two other men said:

'[At the ATC] I'm on screwing at the moment. Screws. I screw in, that's all I do. I like drawing cars you know and houses.'

A man who lives in a co-residency with a family with no handicapped members said:

'I'm a [voluntary] caretaker. I clean up a bit in the community centre before going out. Now and again I go into town.'

A woman who lives alone said of her daily activities:

'I keep myself occupied with him [pointing to a newsreader on the TV who she writes to. She also keeps diaries of when he appears on the TV.] If I get a bit boring I go out for a bus ride or something. I don't like Sundays. They annoy me. It's a boring day. Shops are closed, there's nowhere to go is there? I'd like to get a job because many people now won't accept handicapped people. I'd like to work in a cafe cleaning tables. . . . I used to work in a cafe a long time ago with me sister.'

A man who lives with his partner said:

'I've no intention of bloody working. Why should I?'

In contrast, his partner is disappointed not to have a job.

'I used to work in an old people's home. . . . Well they wanted me to work Christmas eve. Well they wanted me to work for £4 a week. . . . She wanted me to work Christmas eve and Christmas day. I mean £4 a week is not much. . . . I enjoyed working at the old people's home. I enjoyed talking to the old people. We used to have a laugh and a cup of tea . . . but I got the sack so I've got no job at all now. . . . Jim [social worker] has tried to get us a job as a child minder. But you're bored not going out to work. I'm always bored. I started at a night club as a waitress but it was too much. Had to deal with pounds and stuff. . . . I just get fed up because I've not got a job.'

A man who lives alone said:

'I used to go to a training centre [ATC] but I didn't like it so I come to me sister's. I get a bit bored sometimes. . . . I just watch TV all the time. Sometimes I go to the pub. . . . There's nothing else.'

A woman who lives with two female friends described activities at her ATC:

'At the centre we do different things and exercises, PT and reading. And we do about health and things where you look after yourself and all that, like keep your hands clean in case you're living in a house or flat to see how you copes. We do quite a bit at the centre, passes the time.'

A man living with a male friend said:

'One time I went to a training centre [ATC]. I give up. . . . I worked in a signal box before they closed the station. . . . [Now] I do jobs every morning and weekends. . . . I have a look in the shops and there's some that I know in the cafe where I go every day. I have me dinner there. On Friday morning I started going to college again. I'm doing different things.'

A man living alone, works with a team of people in a hospital:

'I'm a gardener. It's very nice.'

A woman who is very keen to be employed, described her daily routine:

'Well sometimes I go and have a look round the shops you know or just have a look round . . . quite often I go to the job centre.'

LEISURE

This section looks at some of the ways people spend their leisure or free time. It is not easy to define leisure although there is general agreement that leisure time and recreational activities are not just ends in themselves. While they provide immediate satisfaction, they are also the means by which we achieve long term personal and social goals (Kelly, 1982). Some researchers suggest that social interaction is one of the most important reasons for, and benefits of leisure (Iso-Ahola and Allen, 1982).

The situation of people who are unemployed and retired deserves particular mention. Unlike employed people or people whose days have some externally imposed structure, they may find it difficult to say when they are engaged in leisure activities. They may also find it difficult to fully occupy their days. It appears that people select the leisure activities with which they feel at ease and are reasonably competent to perform (Iso-Ahola, 1980). However, the financial costs of leisure participation do place major constraints on people with very limited incomes, a characteristic of those who are unemployed and of this population in particular (Wertheimer, 1983).

In this section, the leisure activities that people engage in when they are not in paid work or looking after their homes are considered. Table 4.5 presents details of people's leisure activities. For most people, 'home-based passive' activities refers largely to the television. This heads the list in terms of being a frequent occupation. 'Home-based active' activities vary widely and include drawing, writing, cutting out pictures, watch repair, colouring pictures and bird breeding. Outings are the most frequently cited, non-home-based activity. This may relate to the availability of free travel for people who are disabled in North-West England and also to the increased potential for meeting people. It is clear from Table 4.5 that people enjoy visiting others and that they enjoy having visitors. It is noteworthy that the majority of people (61) were neutral or noncommittal about their leisure activities; 22 people expressed degrees of satisfaction and the responses of only five people were rated as being mildly negative. Only one person expressed a desire to have different leisure activities. In the following quotations a range of people's views are presented.

Table 4.5 *People's leisure activities*

Activity	Number of people
Home-based passive	83
Home-based active	53
Out of house, non-specialist	77
Out of house, specialist (ie. for people with mental handicap)	28
Visiting people*	58
Having visitors*	52
Outings	67
Owning a pet	33
Helping people	16

* Information missing for two people.

The female partner of a couple who are unemployed described their activities:

'We do go and see his brother. We've got no friends really to talk to, discuss or owt. . . . All we're doing is just sitting around the house. . . . Telly is so-so. We just get fed up day in and day out.'

A woman who lives with two female friends, attends an ATC. Her interests are varied:

'I get out and go to clubs [including the specialist Gateway Club]. I go to see Country and Western with a friend who goes to work with me. . . . Can't read very well but I'm picking up very well and I do a bit of reading. . . . It's not so bad. I like knitting. I do knitting to pass the time away. I like knitting and I like children. I go baby minding. I've got relatives with children. I see them quite a bit when I go

home at weekends. . . . I go to the club tonight. They pick us up around 7 o'clock. Things what you do like play tennis or do a little brooch.'

A man who lives alone and attends an ATC described his interests:

'Like television and go walks with Tip [dog], and plants. Like by myself. I lived nine years meself. . . . I'm lucky with plants. Like tapes, listening to stories, yes, Jane Eyre. . . . I make Lego [construction toy].'

A retired woman who lives with a female friend said:

'I like knitting and sewing, painting. . . . I paint out of books and I do a lot of cross stitches.'

A man who lives with three other men and attends an ATC said:

'I go to the pub sometimes. I was there tonight. I have friends in the pub sometimes.'

The male partner of a couple who are unemployed described the activity they enjoy:

'In the good weather we take the dog out most days. We've met a lot of our friends that way. We see people most days that way.'

A man living with a male friend likes sport. He works in sheltered employment.

'Go to me brother's on Monday. I go round there. Play football on Saturdays.'

An unemployed man who lives alone said:

'I have the TV and I watch it and the Ceefax so I can see what I want to watch. I write some things down in my notebooks, the charts and things so I can see what's in the charts. I've always done that. I like the TV. When the Ceefax finishes I go to town and places. I go on the bus with my pass.'

A woman who attends an ATC on a part-time basis and also attends a centre for people who are blind, described her varied activities. Many of these are undertaken with her partner.

'I like going to [Labour] club and bingo and I'm enjoying that . . . went to the library last Friday and I really enjoyed it. And when it's a nice day one Friday we're going out for a cup of tea in a cafe. . . . Go to bingo most of the time. I'm always glad to get out while I can, while I've got the chance. . . . I've made some

friends in the Working Mens' [club] called Kath. It's down the bottom of the road.'

A single man described his activities when he is not at work:

'I go to me mates, I don't stay there too late. I come back and watch the TV or listen to records. I do a lot of cycling. Go all over in the good weather. Not now when it's cold.'

One of two women who are unemployed and share a house said:

'Bingo, we all play really down at the community centre. We go Monday afternoons to bingo, Tuesdays to dominoes and Wednesdays to the raffle and a cup of coffee. . . . We all have our suppers together [with next door neighbours].'

A man who lives alone and attends a centre for people who are partially sighted said:

'I play records and I have my TV. I go to Sally's and Fran's [friends] and they come here sometimes. I made them tea on Sunday. I go to them as well. I like my records a lot, especially Elvis Presley. I've got 32 of his records.

Although some information is missing, it seems that leisure is guided and encouraged by social workers on behalf of 49 people. Classes have been arranged on behalf of nineteen people; and some 39 people have had their holidays arranged for them. In one area, outdoor pursuits were organised. The social worker with responsibility for doing this also helped his clients to save for holidays. As a result, skiing holidays abroad were an important feature of a small number of people's lives.

BIRMINGHAM UNIVERSITY LIBRARY

CLASSIFICATION

The way in which people with mental handicap are frequently described is by reference to their performance on IQ tests. What results from these is an often misleading total score that tends to adhere to people throughout their adult lives. As the total score is a summary of performance on different dimensions, it is uninformative unless the profile of subscores is also considered. This was found to be rarely, if ever, reported in people's case records.

In this study, information concerning 38 people's IQs was derived from IQ measures. Fifteen people were classified as 'borderline', 39 as having 'mild' mental handicap, 23 as having 'moderate' mental handicap and five as having 'severe' mental handicap. Social workers or their predecessors had estimated the

IQ ranges of some 35 people. Information about IQ range was missing for six people in total. Overall, the information regarding people's IQs has to be interpreted with caution. Although there is a widespread use of the IQ in studies of community adjustment, it is important to note that IQs *per se* were not found to be associated with any of the aspects of community adjustment examined in this study.

PEOPLE'S BACKGROUNDS

The concluding section of Chapter 3 reflected that people's lives do not differ vastly from those of their non mentally handicapped neighbours. However, the preceding section on classification reminds us that we must not lose sight of the fact that these people share the label of mental handicap and the educational, training and residential experiences that this entails. Some people's views regarding their label and the implications of this for their lives are presented below. One man living with his partner observed:

'People just get the impression 'cos you're classed as handicapped, bung 'em anywhere. People don't consider, they just stick you anywhere. 'Cos these flats are for bloody elderly. Shouldn't be in here.'

The woman in this relationship is subject to her partner's criticism of her limited skills. She said:

'I can't help it because I don't understand half of the things. See with me working in a special school when I was younger, I never learnt nothing. Me other sisters all went to normal school and because I was slow, they put me in like a slow school and I never learned there.'

One of two women who share a flat said:

'I'm a mencap. Is that the same as being mentally ill? Because when I was 17 my mother was told I had the mental age of nine. I was with her. I'll always think like a child, even though I'm 44. So I've got a split personality. I must have. I've a girl's mind in a woman's body. I've proved myself a woman, with boyfriends and that – but I think like a child. That's what the psychiatrist said. And the psychologist, not long ago said about my IQ [drawing a bell shape in the air] normal people are just here, but you're below it, here . . . I don't seem able to meet Mr Right. Irene [co-resident] says that all we need is a man. But I've had an outside boyfriend, not a mencap like myself, he was a miner and he loved me. He treated me like a daughter, not like a woman. And he said to my mother, "I'll look after your Mary, she's all right." We didn't know he was married. But I proved I was a

woman with him. Slept with him you know. ... . We had a low grade mencap boyfriend. We shared him between us. We felt sorry for him – but he started ripping us off, taking money from us. So we stopped seeing him. ... They put me on the pill because of him. See I can't have any children of my own. But in a way God's given me children. People with Down's syndrome, you know with the Chinese eyes, in the training centre. I love them. Sometimes when they've been crying they come up to me and I love them in my way. So in that way God's given me children, even though I haven't got any.'

A fuller version of this quotation and a consideration of the implications are considered in Flynn and Knussen (1986).

A further example of people's view of their label is provided by a woman whose speech is initially difficult to follow. Her partner's speech can only be understood by her:

'We are handicapped as we left the hostel. We are disabled you know, mentally handicapped they say, don't they? He can't talk properly Paul. It's his speech. There's nobody to teach him to read or write and talk properly. They don't understand. Sometimes I stutter a bit because I got asthma. Makes me can't get me words out properly. I could do with a woman to teach me as well. ... They're very funny some of them. They can't be bothered to understand me you know ... they pick on us 'cause we're mentally handicapped or disabled.'

Finally, a woman who shares a flat with a friend said:

'Some think because you've been in a hostel, you're mental – you're not. I went into a hostel because I couldn't get on with my sister-in-law and I had three mental breakdowns. ... Well people had put it into me head that because I was in hostels, I was mental, but I wasn't. At the time there were no places for people like Christine [co-resident] and me, see. So I had to go into a hostel, they couldn't find places for us. ... I'm good with money but I'm not good with spelling ... so you understand us then, don't you?'

It is clear that the label of mental handicap affects the way in which people see themselves and are seen by others. For many people, this is reinforced by years spent in specialist facilities.

Finally, reference to people's early histories and residential careers can only be of a very general nature. From the information available, it seems that people mostly went into specialist hospitals as children or teenagers and they moved onto hostels, before finally moving into their own homes.

The total number of moves that people have had in staffed and unstaffed accommodation ranges from one to eleven, with an average of five. For 27 people institutions/specialist hospitals were their longest placements and for seventeen people, hostels were their longest placements. While thinking about staffed residential provision for people with mental handicap, it is significant that of the many people who referred to it, all but three described their experiences in hospitals and hostels in a negative way. Of particular concern was the tendency to be treated as children, the absence of privacy and the rules. It is interesting however that a handful of people continue to return to the hostels in which they once lived for assistance with tasks ranging from sewing on buttons to reading letters. Also a small number of people visit their former friends in hospitals. Some 50 people were recorded as being keen to leave staffed accommodation. This picture is consolidated by most of the following quotations concerning hospitals and hostels:

[In hospitals] 'They put me . . . in a hospital place and it was murder.'

'I don't want to go back to the hospital. It was horrible.'

'I wouldn't go back to the hospital. I didn't want to come out though. I was there nearly 50 years, 49 years and 11 months.'

'I've been in and out of hospitals. I've been messed and mucked about ever since I was 31 and I'm 57 this birthday. I've been fed up to the teeth with it. Mrs Cassidy used to be very nice with me. She used to say, "Never mind love one day you'll get out," and I've had my wish.'

'Horrible, weren't it horrible? Used to make you work didn't they?'

'You got fed up. I used to work, work at the potatoes and then I'd be tired.'

'I was in hospital like. I worked in the laundry. I went home every week. She liked it but I didn't. I don't like places like that.'

'I've been in homes and that. Didn't like them so I got out and did [went into] service.'

'I was in hospital 38 years. I was doing nicely, was all right it was, was hospital. You had good doctors, good nurses, good food, good everything. You go to Rhyl, used to go on trips, go all over. It was lovely, 38 years I done there, could have done another 38.'

[In hostels] 'There were too many rules and regulations. You couldn't go to a disco or anywhere you know unless you ask anybody.'

'They used to take your wages . . . they took your bank books as well. I had a stereo and they wouldn't let me have a key for my room. I didn't like that.'

'There was a lad in the hostel called Jack. He's one of these lads who bashes girls up. Anyway, he got me. I didn't like it.'

'I was in that hostel. Awful, no good.'

'The hostel, they help with the bills. Any letters, takes them round there, any letters, electric, gas bills.'

'I used to live in hostel. No like hostel.'

'Lousy. Thought I was never going to get out.'

'Sometimes to get information we go to the hostel. We do a lot ourselves but if we want information we go to the hostel. They explain things you know.'

'When you go back down there, there's nobody really sensible enough to talk to . . . there's only a few can hold a conversation or owt like that. There's only Sally that's sensible really . . . all the others are talking away to themselves.'

'If you don't mind me telling you, I don't care for hostels. That's why I don't want to go into them. I've lived in them and I don't care for them. It's just one of them things.'

'It was all right to rehabilitate you to get you into society but you felt like children again. It was sort of like school.'

'If you need help like sewing, letters I don't understand, you just take them across to the hostel and they explain them to you.'

Lastly, moving on to people's current living circumstances, 38 people continue to live in the tenancies they were first allocated, and 34 people have had only one move. Twelve people have had two moves and seven people have had three or more changes of tenancy. For those who have been living independently for a short time, this instability is worrying.

SUMMARY

The lives of 50 men and 38 women are the focus of this study and their age range is from 22 to 79 years with a concentration of people over the age of 50. In terms of appearance, some people are more noticeable than others because of their weight, the way in which they walk and the poor state of their clothes.

Nineteen people have speech problems. Mild visual problems affect some 26 people and a further three have severe difficulties. Sixteen people experience difficulty walking and thirteen people have epilepsy.

People are largely accomplished in terms of using public transport, dressing appropriately and maintaining proper sleep habits. The skills for which assistance is particularly required are managing finances, paying bills and handling medical problems.

Work is a normal part of adult life and yet jobs are elusive to these people, with only twelve in open employment. Seventeen people attend ATCs, three people are in sheltered employment, three do voluntary work and six people attend Colleges of Further Education. Twenty people are retired and 24 are unemployed, a significant problem in this country. Three people are looking for jobs and eleven people expressed a desire for an ordinary job.

The most frequent occupation of people in their leisure time is watching television. Outings are the most frequently cited non-home-based activity.

The 88 people include fifteen who have 'borderline' mental handicap, 39 who have 'mild' mental handicap, 23 who have 'moderate' mental handicap and five who have 'severe' mental handicap. This information is dated, from a variety of sources and suggests no more than a crude differentiation of people. Although information concerning people's backgrounds is limited, it is clear that the majority of people regard hospitals and hostels in a very poor light.

5
People's Living Circumstances

In order to get a clear picture of how adults with mental handicap who are living independently deal with their everyday lives, it is necessary to know about the conditions in which they live. This chapter begins with a consideration of people's weekly income and moves on to consider the types of housing in which they live. The characteristics of people's neighbourhoods are also presented and undesirable conditions are noted, including the incidence and varieties of victimisation to which some people are exposed. Finally, people's household facilities and belongings are described.

WEEKLY INCOME

As suggested in Chapter 3, some people have pressing needs for financial help. The incomes of 66 people range from £13 to £76, with a low average weekly income of £39 (SD 11.9). These sums refer to the money that people have once deductions have been made at source. (Information about the income of the remaining 22 people was not known by social workers.) Of the information available, it appears that only 23 people have a weekly income that exceeds £40. The Central Statistical Office (1983) showed that in April 1982, the average gross weekly earnings for all full-time, male employees was £150.50. Manual employees earned on average £130.50 and non-manual employees £175.00. Thus people's weekly incomes are low and for some, this imposes serious poverty. This is particularly true of the man whose weekly income is a mere £13. He is paying off a multiplicity of debts each week and is barely able to manage on the sum that remains. He is not alone. Information from case records indicates that 26 people have fuel debts, sixteen people have rent debts and eight people have mail order/hire purchase debts.

People's incomes reflect the fact that they are poorly represented in the workforce. As earnings from employment are the main source of income for most people, these people's financial circumstances differ from those of the majority of people in this country. Only twelve people are in open employment and of these, three are in part-time employment. Also, there are nineteen people in the study over the age of 60, whom we would not expect to be economically active. All but nine people are in receipt of benefits and some people experience extreme deprivation as a result of their limited incomes. This is best conveyed by drawing from interviews with the people concerned. It is surprising that only fifteen people spoke of the difficulties that result from having a limited income. By far the majority of people indicated that their income was 'OK' or 'all right', irrespective of the hardship in which they were living. The following are the experiences of some single people.

> 'They only let me have £13 a week. It's difficult getting by, and I've got bills that I can't pay because I don't have enough. The milkmen keep calling and I have no money. They stopped the papers as well. Peter [social worker] says I've got to pay all the bills I have. It's very hard. . . .'

> 'We get wage, £4 included on that thingy book, supplementary benefit. He'd give you more if he could, but they'd take it out of your book. . . .'

> 'See I don't think I'm getting enough money, I'm only on £35.70 and I don't think it's enough for me. Just because I live on me own and I'm 43 in June or July. Where do you expect a person to live in that way eh? It wouldn't keep me going with this place as well. . . . 'Cos when me mum were alive I used to get more than that, a lot more. . . . It is very hard isn't it?'

> 'Me electric is paid direct now so I've no problems with that. . . .'

It will be seen from the following extracts from interviews that financial poverty is not limited to single people. The following quotations present some of the views of people who live as couples or in groups.

> 'We feel that we could do with a bit more money you know. Like £42 doesn't really go far these days. What we buy out of that is like food, which takes a large part of it like clothing. I just find that I've not bought any clothes for the past three years. Clothes that I see, like I find that I can't afford them anyway. People, shopkeepers, they don't consider the people that are classed as unemployed. . . . What I've been doing is I've been going in the Oxfam shop and I've been getting things fairly cheapish there. . . . I would like, if I could afford it to be able to afford new. Like I'm still in the process of looking for work just at the present moment. I've got clothes but nothing you could call decent like. Like some people say 'I've got a Sunday suit, I wear that for best,' I've not got that. I look on it like it's first impressions like you give to people. It's hopeless going for an office job or something like that dressed up in bloody jeans. Like it's just the prices. We can go out, it just costs money these days, it doesn't matter where you go. See we don't get much money to go out and drink and that. We have a drink one night a fortnight,

so we decide if we stop in this particular night of this week then we go out next week . . . we couldn't afford to go every week . . . Round here they charge you nearly 50p for a loaf of bread, and for 63p you can get two loaves in the big supermarket. In the supermarket the limit is about £20 and we come out with about five carrier bags. If you spent £20 round here you'd get about three carrier bags. It pays to get the white tins [unbranded] with no pictures. You get it cheaper and that way you're getting more. . . .'

'Most days we go into town. We are buying something every week for the baby. Because we're on benefits we've been getting things gradually. . . .'

'Bills love? I wouldn't like to tell you, we don't have any bills. When we pay for the TV licence we have stamps and gas stamps we have and that's all. . . . There's nowhere to go and who wants to go and sit in a picture place? I'm sure I don't, it's too dear anyway. We have to put some money in our bank books every week. She had £200 her and I've got £100 now me. . . .'

'The other problem is getting a licence for this telly. I haven't got the money to do it. I'm frightened if I go to jail or prison any time you know. . . . We share our money . . . they took it away you see. They took the book back for a new one [the DHSS had retained this couple's payment order book]. That's why I've got nothing today . . . I get no food or nothing. I have been without food. It worries me a lot. He's not getting fed properly' [partner].

'We pay the electric, we don't pay the gas because social security pay that for us. We don't pay rent because social security pay that for us. Don't get much to live off do you? He gives me housekeeping money. He has a couple of pounds he pockets. He couldn't sit there with no cigarettes. . . . He takes me out if I haven't got any money left, he'll take me out for a packet of ciggies or a drink. We only go out one day a week though. . . . When I left [work] they said, "When you get married you'll find out what you've got to do . . . you'll find out girl, all about food, rent, electric and gas you've got to pay out. . . ." I found out. It was a shock when I first went out to get the first meal and he came with me. I said "The price of food, we'll have to live on bread and butter." He said "No, we'll live on thin air!"'

These quotations witness the extreme economic hardship of being in receipt of social security benefits. It will be seen in Chapter 7 that social workers are daily concerned with their clients' material needs, fuel poverty, disconnections and general budgeting. Certainly the range of difficulties is large and in some instances, this is a reflection of the preparation people have had. For example, one woman in the early days of residence in her tenancy, tried to pay her gas bill to the window cleaner.

It is noteworthy that budgeting is a skill that largely eludes these people. It will be recalled from Chapter 4 that only 30 people are reckoned to be able to manage their own finances. So some 58 people routinely require help with their money. This task is especially difficult given people's limited incomes.

Some of the harsher consequences of poverty have been outlined in the evidence presented so far: social activities are limited; new clothes are a luxury; and sometimes basic needs are not met. Becker and MacPherson (1986) have shown that income deprivation plays a role in bringing people into contact with social workers and in this respect, these people do not present unique difficulties to social services personnel. It appears that the close link that has been documented between poverty and disability (Durward, 1981; Buckle, 1984; Wilkin, 1979; Baldwin, 1981; Walker, 1981) also operates for adults with mental handicap who are living independently.

HOUSING, OWNERSHIP AND RATEABLE VALUES

Our goal is to see mentally handicapped people in the mainstream of life, living in ordinary houses in ordinary streets, with the same range of choices as any citizen, and mixing as equals with the other, and mostly not handicapped, members of their own community. (Kings Fund Centre, 1980)

Having a decent home, possessions and comforts, and expectations of these for the future is important to our physical and material well being (Flanagan, 1978). Where we live, however, depends on a number of factors, not least of all our income. Neighbourhoods are acknowledged to be broadly segregated by income and thus largely by social class (Rose, 1985; Williams, Sewel and Twine, 1986). To the extent that limited incomes characterise the circumstances of the people I met, it is inevitable that the areas in which some people live are not the most desirable.

It is difficult to measure the quality of housing because it is so multidimensional. Each house is unique and variations relate to tenure, location, size, state of repair, decoration, architectural type, improvements, etc. Tenure is of particular importance in housing. Whether a person buys or rents accommodation, who the property is rented from, affects rights of occupancy, security of tenure, responsibility for repairs and improvements and the extent to which people benefit from appreciation in the value of their home (Department of the Environment, 1980).

Table 5.1 shows the type of houses in which people live; 49 people live in flats in either two-storey or multistorey buildings.

In total 64 people live in council rented housing. Twelve people live in property belonging to the social services and eight people live in housing association property. Two people are owner-occupiers and the remaining two live in private tenancies. The number of people living in flats is high, given that the majority of council tenants live in houses. There is evidence to suggest, however, that the recent entrants to council housing are more likely to live in high flats (Kleinman, Pearce and Whitehead, 1985).

Table 5.1 *People's homes*

Homes	Number of people
Semidetached or detached house	30
First-floor flat in a two-storey building	21
Ground- or first-floor flat in a multistorey building	13
Any other flat in multistorey building	10
Terraced house	6
Ground-floor flat in a two-storey building	5
Semidetached or detached bungalow	3

The rateable value of a property bears 'a reasonable relationship to the other possible indicator of housing quality, sale price, and is available for all dwellings and tenures' (Robinson, O'Sullivan and Le Grand, 1985). It is determined by the characteristics of the dwelling quantity and quality. In principle, they are a measure of the potential rental value of a property but as they are adjusted infrequently, they fall out of line with actual rental values. Although rateable values do not generally take account of environmental features, council housing provides an exception to the rule. These are valued below private sector houses on the grounds that a council estate represents a 'negative' neighbourhood feature. To the extent that houses with comparable rateable values tend to be clustered, they provide a good proxy for the quality of the area as well as the dwelling. Although the information is missing for six households, it will be seen from Table 5.2 that only ten households have rateable values exceeding £200.

Table 5.2 *The rateable value of households*

Rateable values	Number of households	Rateable values	Number of households
£1–£50	2	£151–£200	37
£51–£100	16	£201–£250	7
£101–£150	17	£251–£300	3

Consistently, the homes that were in a poor state of repair were council-rented. This corroborates Purkis and Hodson's (1982) observation that the housing stock is a victim of commercial recession and government cuts and is rapidly falling into disrepair. Byrne *et al.* (1986) confirm this observation and acknowledge that the 'hard to let' estates are particularly associated with council housing. Many of these were built after the Second World War and they have deteriorated rapidly since. Some 38 people live in prewar housing and 50 in postwar housing. Seventeen people live in council estates of multistorey buildings, 29 live in areas of council housing alone and only 42 people live in areas of private and non-council housing; 22 people in total live in tenancies that may be described as 'hard to let'. Of these, fourteen people live in flats on estates that are bywords for vandalism, deprivation and crime. Of such estates, Byrne *et al.* (1986) make the following observations:

The dwellings themselves have deteriorated and the environment has become increasingly barren and deprived physically and socially. As the estates have acquired an undesirable reputation, so no one but the most desperate has been prepared to accept tenancies. Thus deprivation is intensified, with a concentration of households with social and economic difficulties. (p. 38)

This issue is highlighted if cues to the quality of people's immediate neighbourhoods are considered. Following Davie *et al.* (1982), Johnston (1981), Dahman (1983, 1985) and Duncan (1971), the presence or absence of three aspects of the environment that are symptomatic of deterioration were noted: boarded-up or disused houses/flats are close to the homes of sixteen people; uncollected rubbish has accumulated near the homes of twelve people; and graffiti appear on walls and buildings near sixteen people's homes. One man rarely leaves his flat in order to ensure that it is not broken into and vandalised. This is the usual fate of his neighbouring flats.

At this point it is appropriate to consider some people's views about their homes and neighbourhoods. One man who lives on the sixth floor of deck access flats observed:

'I've been burgled three times. The first time, I hadn't got very much in it. Even after that there's never been very much to take. I've got a good door now, though I told them to come and change the windows.'

One of two sisters sharing a flat said:

'I like living here best. Don't get no trouble at all here. The neighbours are all right. . . . I always wanted a place of me own.'

Two brothers living on the second floor of deck access flats noted:

'It's not too bad. We've lived in worse. This is the best one we've had. Even though it's cold and there's a draught by the window. It's somewhere to go.'

A single man said of his ground-floor flat:

'See it's all damp in here, damp: . . .'

An elderly woman who lives alone said of her flat:

'It's nice living in it. I can cook and do everything. . . . I had it painted out just when I came in it. I like to keep it the best way I can. I dry them [clothes] outside on the balcony. The balcony is half and half. The gentleman next to me has it as well and there's a gate. I look down on the sea and you can go down and sit down.'

A couple were disappointed with their first-floor flat for the following reason:

'I wanted a downstairs floor one and they put us darn well upstairs. Right near a tree and the trouble is we get interference on the TV.'

A single elderly woman described the block in which she lives:

'They're nice new flats.'

A couple who have lodgers said of their deck access flat:

'It's noisy here. They've got children down there and some flats are empty. I'm not bothered. It's a roof over me head. They said they were pulling these flats down but I don't think they are.'

A single man, resident in a first-floor flat, said of the estate in which he lives:

'Terrible place you know. They do some terrible things here.'

A single woman who lives in a ground-floor flat noted:

'You get used to people shouting, people banging on doors and kids coming up smashing windows.'

A single man, the tenant of a semi-detached house said:

'I like it round here. It's lovely but the garden, I don't want to be messin' around with that.'

A couple who live in a ground-floor flat outlined their reason for wanting to move:

'We've been trying to move but I don't think there's much chance of it. It's not the place, it's the people what live round here. I'd like to move out if I could get back to where I came from . . . we've sent forms in and forms in and nothing's happened . . . any chance of getting us out of here?'

A woman who shares a flat with her female friend said:

'See in the flat you can relax, do anything. Everybody likes it . . . even the handyman said it was nice and tidy. . . . The nurse comes now and then to check our tablets and she says, "I don't like going out of this flat, I'm so comfortable!"'

An elderly man, the resident of a seventh-floor flat in a tower block said:

'It's not a nice area and the Housing said they can't shift me to sheltered accommodation. And the council turned round and said stop where I am, you know what I mean? They told me I could find me own place. . . .'

With some of these observations in mind, it is not surprising that one social worker advised me not to visit her client in his flat in the evenings. She recommended that I should make arrangements to meet him either at his place of work or in the social services department. In total 38 people said positive things about their living circumstances and only fifteen were neutral on the subject; 31 people expressed dissatisfaction and of these, seventeen said they wanted to move. Researchers have found that if people are satisfied with their homes they are also likely to be satisfied with their neighbourhoods (Galster and Hesser, 1981). Although the desire to change or move homes is not always associated with people's negative views about their housing situation (Ginsberg and Churchman, 1984), for the people I met this was consistently the case.

Williams, Sewel and Twine (1986) have investigated the distribution of tenants with different incomes in council housing. They found that tenants are not randomly distributed throughout council housing stock. It emerges that tenants with low incomes (under £50) are, 'more likely to be living in the less desirable parts of the housing stock, whether defined by dwelling type or estate, and tenants with high incomes (£100 or over) are more likely to be in the more desirable parts of the stock'. Given that exactly a quarter of the study population reside in 'hard to let' tenancies, and that 55 people in total have weekly incomes of less than £50, it is not surprising that some people have been allocated poorer quality homes in undesirable areas.

VICTIMISATION

Victimisation is a further dimension of the quality of people's neighbourhoods. Table 5.3 presents information from people's case records on the extent of this for the people I met. The column on the right presents the number of people for whom information is missing.

Table 5.3 *Victimisation*

Type of victimisation	Number affected	Missing
Intimidation from children	22	3
Property stolen/financially 'milked'	17	8
Intimidation from neighbours	15	5
Home and property damaged	12	8
Exploited by non-family member	10	5
Exploited by family member	6	3
Mugging/physical abuse	2	6

During the interviews I did not specifically ask about the experience of being victimised. The following quotations arose spontaneously as people described their homes and neighbourhoods. It will be gathered that some people are 'repeat victims', that is, their experiences are not isolated incidents in their lives. They appeared bewildered and despondent when describing their experiences. The quotations indicate how some people are victimised, how some struggle to make sense of the trauma, how some people act to protect themselves against future intrusion, and somehow, carry on. A single man described the activities of his neighbours:

'That fella downstairs was bunging my keyhole up. I told the social worker about it. He wouldn't do that to anybody else. . . . I got beaten up in the other place. Three fellas broke in . . . they make a fool of you all the time you know, kids. People that go in the shop treat you like a fool you know. It's an awful feeling you know . . . it's not a joyride. . . .'

A single man was in hospital with malnutrition following an unscrupulous neighbour taking his food and money:

'I didn't see any of me money or any of me food. I didn't see a thing . . . all I used to get back was about £2 you know, and that was out of £36. You can imagine where the £34 was going to you know . . . that was going on for a while, which I didn't tell Angela [social worker]. . . . I was a bit scared actually telling Angela about it you know at the time but I was going thinner and thinner you know and I couldn't get into any of the clothes . . . I couldn't eat a thing. All I could eat was soup. . . .'

A single woman has a particularly difficult time in her neighbourhood:

'One time when I got my money a man followed me and I took a short cut back and he got me against a wall, beat me and took my purse. . . . I don't have many fits now. I do when anything happens that upsets me. Like when I was mugged, and when I've been robbed. I've been robbed three times in two years here. That's why I always keep my curtains closed. . . . This [flat] is all I could get. I'd like to move because of the kids. They throw eggs and all sorts at my windows. They call me names and throw things at me when I'm out. The window cleaner can't get the mess off the windows. The police can't do anything about it. No one can stop them. My brother always walks me back if I go out. . . .'

One man, the youngest in a group home of four people described the following incidents:

'Some weeks ago there's lads and girls messing about here and they knocked on our door and said, 'Can we come in for a brew?' They just come in and made us *make a brew for them. And there's girls hanging around the bus stop and when I'm taking Kathleen home and Mick's taking Maura, they say "Yer spastics," all that carry on, swearing at us and I don't like it. I can't go up and hit them, I can't. Ignore them? Some kids are all right, some kids let on to me. . . .'*

One man who lives alone, moved to another flat to avoid being plagued by youngsters:

'I prefer this place because there was a lot of trouble over in Lowther Road. You know, all the lads from round there, they kept coming in. They smashed all me records up, broke me record player, broke me bed and that by jumping on it. . . .'

A single man described himself and one of the difficulties he has with local youngsters:

'I'm what's called mentally handicapped, a bit slow. I have some problems with the local kids. They say, "Out the way fatso. . .".'

A woman described the attentions she and her husband attract from local children:

'I'm not happy with the kids, children. They can't understand me, that's why they do this to me. They throw all muck on me windows, smashing me windows every night, causing trouble, sending me up. . . . There's no one to listen to me or give me help or something . . . they give me hassle. I do get a lot of hassle. All me windows get smashed. . . . I shouldn't be here the police say . . . it's a very bad place, a bad place for me. I been knocked about. I hate it. The place itself would be all right if you got rid of the children, all the bullies. . . . I get frightened here . . . It's a terrible world. I get belted up and all sorts. There are fifteen schools round here. They want to belt you or break your jaw in 'cause they hate you. . . . My fella, he goes out and does the shopping because I'm scared of the children. . . . I'm nervy and frightened . . . they skit at me, at me stomach and me legs . . . you're by yourself like. They pick on us 'cause we can't talk properly and we're mentally handicapped or disabled . . . that's why they pick on me. . . .'

A couple described what happens to them in their neighbourhood:

'I don't know why they just pick on us, nobody else here, just us. They've always done it, ever since we've lived here. It's nearly always different ones all the time . . . I've closed the curtains a few times and they've smashed me windows in. A pellet came through the window on New Years Eve. It's a good job I moved out of the way quick or I'd have had a big lump of glass in me back. . . . Sometimes they take your washing off the line . . . you can't put any thing out round here . . . It's disgusting, I hate it. I don't mind the flat, it's just the area that I can't settle in. I'm

*dreading every night. I sit and watch telly and they're banging the window . . .
The police are here more times than they're not. I think they're fed up of seeing us
the police . . . why do kids do it to some people and not to others? They've never
bothered with that girl over the road or any of the others, it's always us . . .'*

Fischer and Wertz (1979) suggest that the experience of being victimised makes
people see others as predators and themselves as prey. People who are victimised
experience, 'vulnerability, separateness, and helplessness in the face of the callous, insensitive, often anonymous enemy'. From their investigation of the recol-
lections of some 50 victims' experiences, they propose that '. . . the victim finds
him/herself pervasively attuned to the possibility of victimisation'. Further, they
suggest that people may recover some sense of order in their lives, '. . . through
considering or taking precautions against crime, usually by restricting one's range
of activities so as not to fall prey again . . .'.

Of the people I met, 29 have experienced some form of victimisation as listed in
Table 5.3, 22 have experienced two or more forms, and twelve people three or
more forms. It is horrifying that one person has been subject to all forms of
victimisation. There is no evidence to indicate that the experience of being
victimised is any less harrowing for people with mental handicap than anybody
else. Inevitably, not everybody discussed the experience of being victimised.
Perhaps it is a phenomenon that will always be underreported, as for some people
it is too distressing and personally discrediting to recall. Some people may not
even be aware of its more subtle forms, as in the case of the social worker who is
suspicious that her client's neighbours are stealing money from him. The man
concerned gives his neighbours money every week to cook five evening meals for
him. They often accompany him when he goes shopping. He has only praise for his
neighbours. Another social worker knows that the friend of one of his clients is
lightfingered. He also knows that his client derives a great deal from this
friendship and is disinclined to suggest that the association should cease.

Everybody interviewed who detailed experiences of being victimised perceived
that the victimisers are in the wrong. In spite of this awareness, they have struggled
on, sometimes without informing their social workers until it is too late. There
appeared to be overwhelming frustration that faith in control over one's life is
misplaced and that friendliness amongst neighbours for example, cannot be taken
for granted.

Against such a backcloth, what of the necessary excursions to local shops, the
launderette and telephone? Conscious of the incidence of victimisation for the
study population, I noted the walking time from people's homes to their nearest
facilities. Proximity to a telephone and launderette is unimportant for the 27 and
49 people respectively who own 'phones and washing machines. In respect of telephones, 37 people have less than a ten-minute walk and 24 people have a walk in
excess of ten minutes. Many telephones had been vandalised. The people without
washing machines fare rather less well. Only eight people have to walk for less
than ten minutes to get to their nearest launderette. The remaining 31 have a walk

of over ten minutes. A fortunate 52 people live close to their food/general stores, but for 36 people the walk to their nearest is more than ten minutes.

Only three people in the study have transport. Two men cycle to work daily and one of these men has a licence for a motor bike. Another man has a moped. Most people with a disability in the North-West travel free on public transport.

While this information may appear very detailed, given that 29 people are subject to some form of victimisation, absences from their home may be so frightening that they do not go out as often as they should or would like. Kail and Kleinman (1985) have shown that the quality of life in urban areas has been affected by crime and fear and by self-imposed restrictions on daily routines. Some people take precautions and only leave their homes when youngsters are unlikely to be around. Others ensure that they or their partners always have an escort when they leave their homes. Three people always keep their curtains closed, irrespective of the time of day, in order not to encourage the unwanted attentions of taunting children and/or burglary. Such considerations affect and limit people's necessary daily routines.

HOUSEHOLD FACILITIES AND LIVING CIRCUMSTANCES

Moving on to consider the fabric and amenities of people's homes, the availability of these is often regarded as an indicator of quality. Townsend (1979) suggests that in order to locate households on a continuum of deprivation/privilege, household facilities and belongings should be noted. Thus the average number of rooms per household is five (SD 1.2; range two to eight), and the average number of rooms heated during the winter is five (SD 1.7; range one to seven). Everybody has a bathroom and a kitchen and everybody has electricity. At the time of interviewing, one man did not have running hot water, but he was the only person I met without this. The homes of a small group of people are in a poor state of repair. Seven people's homes are plagued with rising damp, ten have loose brickwork, and ten at least one badly fitting window. The majority of people's homes, however, are in a reasonable state of repair.

Table 5.4 presents details of people's household facilities and contrasts these with facilities available in all households as reported by the Central Statistical Office (1983). It will be seen that nearly everybody has a television and fridge and in this respect they closely resemble most households. Most people have carpets covering all or nearly all of the floor in their main sitting-room and most people have enough comfortable seating in their homes for all occupants plus one visitor. It is interesting that more people in this study have central heating than people in other households. In contrast, fewer people have vacuum cleaners and fewer have washing machines when compared with other households. Only 31 per cent of people in this study have their own 'phones and this is significantly fewer than most other households. Arguably this reflects the inadequate financial resources people have at their disposal.

Table 5.4 *People's household facilities*

Resource	Percentage of people with these	CSO (1983) (%)
Carpets on nearly all the floor in main sitting-room	99	–
Television	98	97
Fridge	95	93
Comfortable seating for occupants plus one visitor	94	–
Radio	94	–
Vacuum cleaner	74	95
Central heating	66	59
Washing machine	56	79
Telephone	31	76

Obviously, facilities can only be described as such if people are able to operate them and/or meet the costs. It is noteworthy that one woman had had her telephone cut off because she is unable to meet her phone bill of over £100. While she acknowledges that she did not always use it wisely (she lives alone and is lonely), she is afraid that in the event of having an epileptic fit she will be unable to summon assistance. In the interim, she is paying off her debt at £1 per week. One man does not know how to operate his central heating system. His flat is damp and he chooses to sit and eat mostly in his kitchen which is heated by a small electric fire.

In Chapter 7 it will be seen that one of the main activities of social services personnel is that of monitoring the cleanliness of people's homes. Given this preoccupation, it was decided to take note of cleanliness and use the resulting information as an outcome measure. Using a scale developed by Davie *et al.* (1982), details were recorded after the interview – in other words, not in people's homes. Often people gave me guided tours but I did not request these. This explains the extent of the missing information. Reference to Table 5.5. suggests that a small number of people experience difficulty in keeping their homes clean.

Table 5.5 *The cleanliness of people's homes*

Items rated	Present	Absent	Missing
Floor covering soiled, covered in bits	25	63	–
Smell	19	69	–
Kitchen sink, draining board and surfaces have not been washed for a long time	4	79	5
Bath, basin or toilet showing ingrained dirt	4	65	19
Kitchen appliances and implements showing remnants of food from previous meals	3	79	6

SUMMARY

Financial poverty characterises the circumstances of the people in this study; sixty-six people have a low average weekly income of £39 (range £13–£76), with 55 people in receipt of sums of less than £50.

Most people live in council-rented housing and over half live in flats in either two-storey or multistorey buildings; twenty-two people live in 'hard to let' tenancies and the homes of fourteen people are in especially undesirable areas.

Victimisation in a variety of forms impinges on the lives of 29 people in total. Some people's accounts of their experiences, within and outside their homes are harrowing. Some talked of the fear they feel outside their homes and yet only three people have their own transport. Not everybody is well situated in terms of local amenities.

Regarding household amenities, most people are fairly well served. Over half have a washing machine, and over a quarter their own telephones. A small number of people experience difficulty in keeping their homes clean.

Importantly, people are very moderate in terms of their views about their weekly incomes with only five people expressing a desire for an increase in their incomes. In contrast, people's homes evoked a broader range of views with seventeen people wishing to move.

6

The Social Environment

The majority of the 88 people whose lives are the subject of this study have lived in hospitals and hostels for long periods. They have been 'returned to the community' or rather their areas of origin at a time of expanding unemployment, the decline of inner city neighbourhoods and a shift in policy towards greater reliance on the resources of the community (Barclay, 1982).

Against this background, this chapter looks at people's social environments and their views regarding these. Firstly, it considers the importance of social networks and goes on to look at living arrangements, the experience of living alone, the roles of partners and children, co-residents, families, and neighbours.

SOCIAL NETWORKS AND SOCIALISATION

There is a vast body of research regarding the value and benefits of support from our social networks. These are regarded as a resource which helps us to cope with stress and overcome its debilitating effects. Social support has been reported to protect against depression (for example, Brown and Harris, 1978; Surtees, 1980; Billings and Moos, 1981) and against mental illness and psychological distress (for example, Miller and Ingham, 1976; Williams, Ware and Donald, 1981; Lin and Dean, 1984; Gottlieb 1985); it is reported to reduce stress in work and unemployment (for example, Gore, 1978; House, 1981); and generally to alleviate illness (for example, Lin *et al.* 1979; Asher, 1984). While there are methodological problems in the literature regarding social support (Starker, 1986), the conclusion that it is critical to well-being is unavoidable. In brief, the present state of knowledge suggests that social support moderates the damaging effects of stressful life events and is related to good health.

Without question, in times of need, our personal networks (that is, the web of social ties that surround us) and social activities can be important sources of support, information and material assistance, regardless of how we are labelled. For people with mental handicap, however, difficulties may arise as a result of a limited grasp of the skills necessary for social behaviour and social relationships. By definition, a person with mental handicap is impaired in the effectiveness with which she/he '. . . meets the standards of personal independence and social responsibility expected of his/her age and cultural group' (Grossman, 1975).

Nobody is born with an understanding of appropriate behaviour. This is culturally determined and passed on. People with mental handicap are denied many of the socialising experiences to which non mentally handicapped people are exposed. Edgerton (1975) illuminates this fact with the description of a man who was labelled as having a mental handicap at the age of four. At the age of eighteen years, the man was discovered to have an IQ of 104. He was ill-prepared for an independent life and in his own words observed that it was 'much easier to be retarded'. This sobering case study prompted Koegel (1978) to report, '. . . it would appear that the socialization process undergone by mentally retarded people leaves even a normal individual ill-equipped for participation in normal networks' (p. 8).

At this point, it is timely to reflect upon the implications of normalisation for association with others. Perhaps it is 'culturally normative' to encourage association with non mentally handicapped people and discourage association with other devalued individuals. It appears misguided, however, to hope that friendships can develop with non mentally handicapped people and to aspire to this for everybody. Friendships have a longitudinal perspective and social, attitude and value similarity affect friendship formation (Baker, 1983). It is to be expected that people who have spent vast periods of their lives associating with people with mental handicap will form friendships with them. Discouraging these friendships implies that we do not value them.

In this study, people's social networks were considered too complex an issue to address within the timescale of three years. In the pilot study it appeared that some people's understanding of friendships was limited. For example one woman told her social worker that she had sent over 200 Christmas cards to her 'best friends'. Following a December meeting of two hours' duration with this woman, I also received a Christmas card addressed, 'To my very, very best friend with lots of love from your very, very best friend.' The card was covered in kisses. Following discussion with social workers, we reflected that questions concerning friends may produce an unrealistic impression of people's networks (an observation subsequently confirmed by Luckman, 1986). Consequently, a request to 'Tell me about who comes to see you/who you go to see' replaced one regarding friendships. Although there is a strong possibility that this has resulted in underreporting (Sigelman *et al.*, 1982), I believe that the picture that has emerged is more valid than it might have been otherwise.

Information about people's social environments was derived from social workers' observations and those of their clients. Social workers estimated that 62 people had regular contact with their friends (including people with mental handicap and non mentally handicapped people); eleven people had intermittent contact; four people had no contact; and four social workers did not know about their clients' contact with friends. This information was missing for seven people in total.

Of the people themselves, some 71 people talked of contact with others (often describing individuals as 'friends'), but frequently they referred to social services or community mental handicap team personnel. Some 54 people talked of visiting others, but once again this included social workers as well as people unassociated with services, including families. In terms of satisfaction, twenty people appeared positive about their contact with others, and only five were rated as making remarks implying dissatisfaction. One person expressed a desire to have a very different social environment (and she is described in Chapter 3). In total, however, 59 people made noncommittal or neutral comments about their contact with others, such as *'She comes to see me and I see her and it's OK. . . . All right, we go out sometimes, that's all.'*

The resulting picture is difficult to interpret as the information gathered from the two sources is not directly equivalent. Also, variables such as age, duration of stay in hospitals and hostels, contact primarily with services and/or families, the consequences of living alone or living with others could not be teased out from descriptive and interview material alone. Ostensibly, however, it appears that most people have regular contact with individuals who may be described as friends. However, we must not lose sight of the fact that a number of people experience loneliness and isolation. According to social workers, four people had no contact with friends and eleven only had intermittent contact. In the interviews eighteen people did not mention contact with others. As the recipient of two marriage invitations and many requests for further contact with the people I met, I have to conclude that some people's networks are wanting.

PEOPLE'S LIVING ARRANGEMENTS

In line with the social support literature, Alwin, Converse and Martin (1985) suggest that the make-up of a person's household defines and constrains the contact she/he has with others and has consequences for emotional and psychological well-being. Looking at marriage, for example, a number of studies suggest that married people (with intact marital relationships) enjoy greater amounts of satisfaction and psychological well-being than unmarried people (Gurin, Veroff and Feld, 1960; Campbell, Converse and Rogers, 1976). Further, it is believed that unmarried people experience more stress in their lives as a consequence of their isolation (Kessler and Essex, 1982). There are gender differences, however, in the degree of stress afforded by marriage. Among elderly people, women who have never married are better off than married women and they in turn are happier than widowed women (Taylor and Ford, 1983).

Moving on to consider living arrangements, Table 6.1 shows that most people live with one or more than one other person – that is, 26 people live alone, 37

Table 6.1   *People's living arrangements*

	Males	Females	Total
Living alone	17	9	26
Living with somebody else:			
Marriage partner/cohabitee	9	9	18
Sister/brother	2	2	4
Parent/child	2	–	2
Friends	6	7	13
Living with two others	4	6	10
Living with three others	8	4	12
Living with more than three others	2	1	3
Total	50	38	88

people live with one other person and 25 people live with two or more others. Although the extent of people's involvement with the decision that they should leave hospitals and hostels is not known, with odd exceptions, these living arrangements do reflect the active preferences of the people themselves. The exceptions include three people who have been divorced and a group home of four men who were not consulted about the selection of their co-residents. Aligned with this, a woman described in Chapter 3 was lonely and saddened that she was unable to share her flat with a male friend many years her senior. Staff had informed her that she would lose her income if her friend moved into her flat.

In total, 77 people originated from the North-West and the remaining eleven from areas throughout the United Kingdom. Current residence in the North-West can be explained by family migration, transfers during periods in staffed accommodation and requests during periods in staffed residences to live with friends from other areas.

The Central Statistical Office (1983) has shown that the percentage of people living alone has more than doubled, from 4 per cent in 1961 to 9 per cent in 1982. The increase in single households is attributed to the increased longevity of people, especially women, into old age. Certainly the likelihood of living alone increases with age. In this respect, the living arrangements of the people I met are not typical as some 30 per cent of people live alone and most of these people are neither elderly nor female.

Other important differences concern the number of two person households. Some 20 per cent of people are married or live with partners; 38 people in total (43 per cent) live with their friends. This contrasts strikingly with 8 per cent of people in Great Britain in 1982 living with unrelated persons. The majority of people live in families headed by a married couple (Central Statistical Office, 1983).

In the sections that follow, extracts from the interviews are presented. In 'Living alone', the quotations largely concern people's views about their living arrangements and the contacts they have with others. In 'Partners and children', the interview extracts focus largely upon people's views about shared lives and suggest something of the immediate support that is available. 'Co-residents' explores both in-house and external relationships.

LIVING ALONE

Of the 26 people in the study who live alone, one woman is divorced, and the remainder have never been married. For some people, the isolation of living alone is a cause of deep dissatisfaction. This is particularly the case where contact with friends or services is limited. For example, one man is acknowledged to have a drinking problem and he has little contact with anybody but his brother's family. His social worker appreciates that his client is lonely and that he enjoys the conviviality of a pub. Another man who has no friends, excites the concern of local ATCs because of his homosexuality. His social worker is worried about her client's expressed loneliness and is immersed in the uphill task of trying to alter the intolerance of ATC staff towards homosexuality. Her client is very shy and cannot make friends easily.

Not everybody who lives alone is socially isolated. As Hughes and Gove (1981) observed, living alone causes some people to compensate for the absence of immediate social support by developing a greater degree of contact with friends. For people who have lived in hospitals and hostels, contact with friends is almost consistently contact with other people with mental handicap.

One man, who is in sheltered employment, said of his living situation:

'I like it. I see my friends when I want to and I can do what I want when I'm here. I go to Pam's [friend from hostel] when I feel like it. I see friends but I like being here.'

A woman who has a part time job said, *'I've got me friends in work'*. She is a very active member of the women's group in her local church and she has a photo of the vicar and his family in her living room. Every couple of months she stays with a family (arranged by the social services department) for weekends and holidays. She enjoys their company and their children. She was distressed that her social worker of five years had recently moved:

'When he left me I was really depressed . . . I cried me eyes out. [At church] they're friendly there, I go Sunday morning and Saturday night. They go out of the church to picnics and we have a harvest festival. We do give them a hand out. We have a harvest supper. . . . I've had a friend I went with called Meg. She's left now but I've got a penfriend of her. . . . The family are awful nice. I went there for a holiday for a week and the little girl said, "I want you to stay here, I don't want you to go home." My friend Jan does the [church] flowers. She goes to the church and tells me when it's my turn. . . . I'm off to a "Lift Meeting" [at church], it's

only up the road. Something to do with ladies only . . . just have cups of tea and sing songs. . . . Last Sunday at church we had some lovely slides and all sorts of Hong Kong and China and all different countries. . . . When I came here the vicar took me up to see the church and he brought me home. . . .'

A woman in her mid-50s has been living in her locality for some 20 years. She was recently made redundant. An elderly friend whom she visited daily and nursed in ill-health died some weeks prior to our meeting.

'People here are sociable. Everybody in the shops know me. Nobody doesn't know me . . . [The flat] it's nice living in it. I can cook in it and do everything . . . I have a fella coming round sometimes. He comes round to see me. There's no harm in having a boyfriend is there? [Absent from her flat during the day] I don't come back 'till late, I visit different people. See I go out and enjoy myself while I can, while I got the chance. But when you get older you won't be able to do it the same . . . Somebody said to me why don't I go and live with my friend, the one who died. And I said, I wouldn't always have her and I'd have to try and manage on me own two feet . . . Some people don't like living on their own do they? I like it because I'm out most of the time and I see people around the town. It's not like I don't see people. And they're all friendly round here so that's the way I like it. I social work them and they social work me . . . Two ladies from the laundrette bought me him [a budgie] for Christmas. . . .'

An unemployed woman who lives in a ground-floor flat has been subject to a lot of harassment from children. She has put on a lot of weight since leaving the hostel. Her social worker appreciates that she overeats because she is bored.

'It's great isn't it living on your own. . .? They keep telling me to lose weight but what do I do? Carry on eating. . . . George [a former hostel resident] comes to my house. I go to his to see if he's all right. He wants company. He's on his own, he gets bored. . . . Me phone's not on at the moment. I've had a lot of problems with that. . . . I've had a big bill, £108. . . . Sitting around here and looking at the cat all the time is nothing.'

One man who is in full-time employment would like to live in a small flat. He currently lives in a three-bedroomed terraced house with a large back garden. He said of his living circumstances:

'Me mum died you see. . . . I only live in this part [of the house], I don't bother with the other part. . . . I sleep in here [living room]. . . . I feel lonely up there. . . . I go to me sister's sometimes like. They mostly come here . . . only me brother and me sister and me social worker come to see me . . . but I have no friends of me own like. At work, yes mostly male friends. I'm a bit shy with girls. But most of the men have left, they're all new ones and they don't know me as much.'

An elderly man living in a block of flats in an area of 'hard to let' tenancies said:

'I get a bit lonely sometimes when I'm on me own in a way. It worries me, and I can't go out on buses when it's bad at night, [this is] not a nice area. . . . I was going to me sister's tomorrow. . . . I go every fortnight. I come back at night . . . she wouldn't come here to see me. . . . They don't bother with you the neighbours here. . . . Nobody comes to see me at all. I don't know. Nobody comes and see how I'm getting on. . . .'

PARTNERS AND CHILDREN

Clearly these 88 people are different from non mentally handicapped people in so far as they are less likely to be living in families and to have their own families. To understand this, it is necessary to reflect on their socialising experiences and the caution that attends the issue of marriage and parenthood for people with mental handicap. Only nine people in the study have not lived in any form of staffed residential accommodation. A number of people have spent most of their lives in institutions, some of whom were institutionalised because they were labelled 'moral imbeciles' and were believed to be in danger of being sexually exploited. Their segregation, 'reflected the community and professional fear that the mentally retarded would beget the mentally retarded' (Haas, 1979). Away from their families some people have experienced multiple residential placements, and inevitably this has affected their opportunities to make and keep relationships.

A powerful argument in suppressing close friendships amongst people with mental handicap is that they may lead to sexual relationships, and an active sexual life requires a degree of responsibility and maturity beyond these people. But attitudes and policies are changing, there are ever-increasing numbers of people living in community settings and the negative features of strict control in institutional settings are being replaced by attempts to foster more socially appropriate behaviour (Pitceathly and Chapman, 1985). Whittemore and Koegel (1978) observe that leading as normal a life as possible must result in acceptance of the tenet that healthy social and sexual relationships are basic to a person's adaptation to community life.

Marriage and parenthood enter people into new social relationships and a few studies have looked at people with mental handicap in these roles. Of marriage, researchers have indicated its importance in enhancing self-esteem, providing companionship and enabling couples to be more independent and self-sufficient than they could manage living separately (Mattinson, 1970; McCarver and Craig, 1974; Floor, Baxter and Zisfein, 1975; Craft and Craft, 1979). There are three married couples in the population of 88 and a further six couples are living together. One such couple is described in Flynn (1987), and another in Chapter 3. One couple were expecting a baby at the time of interview and one man is a single parent. A single woman had an abortion several years ago.

Research regarding people with mental handicap as parents produces a rather clouded picture. Their abilities to provide appropriate environmental stimulation for their children's development, to perceive their children's needs and deal effectively with misbehaviour for example, are concerns. Mattinson (1970) noted that when parenting problems arose, these tended to be due to factors other than IQ, such as family size and socioeconomic status. In a study of two families, Winik (1982) found that parents experienced difficulties in coping once their child became verbal and active; they tended not to be aware of problems, and sorting out daily concerns was as much as they could manage. She concluded that people need an extensive amount of support to facilitate parenting. In contrast, Johnson (1969) proposed that the rights of a child should be paramount and wonders whether parenthood is the 'automatic right of all human beings'. Mindful of the possibility of non mentally handicapped children becoming precociously competent, O'Neill (1985) underlined the importance of '. . . the presence, duration and quality of the parents' social support. School and social agency supportive contacts with retarded parents are encouraged because these people are at risk from adjustment problems' (p. 267).

The experience of being married/having a partner and being a parent must be gathered from the following accounts and observations. In the study, no attempt was made to assess the quality of people's relationships or the adequacy of parenting skills. Information was gleaned from contact with social workers, case records and the interviews themselves.

For example, Mr and Mrs Heaton are desperately unhappy with their flat and neighbourhood as they have been exposed to physical and verbal abuse. They go to their neighbours in time of distress and keep in contact with both of their families. They are both unemployed. Mrs Heaton reflected on their lives together and the roles they have:

'He gives me the housekeeping money . . . he takes me out. If I haven't got any money left, he'll take me out for a packet of ciggies or a drink. . . . He used to help me with the shopping a lot, because I got cataracts on me eyes, I can't see. I can't see across the road now. He's got to come with me and take me everywhere. . . . I can manage round in the house, do the washing and that. . . . I don't like asking a man to wring me underclothes, but he wrings all me other stuff out like sheets. . . . I do me work, tidy up here and just put the telly on and watch it. . . . If I do the bedroom, he'll do in here for me you know, brush up and wash around. . . . He decorated this, he helps, he's a good fella . . . if he wasn't happy with me he wouldn't come back. . . . Are you married? Take my advice, don't!'

Mr Bowland and Miss O'Brien are looking forward to the birth of their first child. They see Miss O'Brien's family regularly and are gradually meeting people in their own locality. Miss O'Brien is trying to overcome her shyness with the help of her partner and social worker. Both unemployed, Mr Bowland shares all the household tasks. He said:

'I've made the tables, they taught me how to make things like that at the centre [for people with epilepsy]. I also do the decorating. I've done all of this flat. . . . We're going to the hospital once a week to the antenatal clinic. There's a launderette nearby and we take the washing at weekends. . . . We were both at the centre and they teach you how to do lots of things there, that's men and women. So while we can both cook, I do it mostly, especially now that Joan's having a baby.'

Mr Rangecroft and Miss Watson share their flat with two lodgers. They have few contacts with people outside their flat. They are both unemployed and share many of the household tasks:

'We do the cooking, cleaning and laundry together. Do shopping on Saturdays once a fortnight. We both go to the shops. We do washing [laundry] in the bath. I don't know how long we've been together, on and off. We met at the hostel. . . .'

Mr Walker and Miss Cooke are anxious to leave their flat. They are unemployed and bored with being at home most days. They have had arguments with their friends and now have no friends on whom they can call. Mr Walker has strong views about his partner's appearance. He also regrets her sterilisation:

'It's only bloody right that women should dress up. I mean bloody men just stick anything on. It's only right you dress up. . . . See we want a child. I've got nephews and that and they say if we're on the bus, 'Look Uncle Ben, look . . .! Well it's not the same as 'Look dad, look . . .! She's going to see if she can have the operation reversed.'

Mr Longton and Miss Madoc live in an attractive flat on a modern estate. They have busy social lives and enjoy meeting friends at the local pub. They are both in full-time employment and share the housework. Miss Madoc said:

'I like living with Joe. I can get to work easily and get home and it's near for Joe. I look after Joe. I mean, we fall out, but we all do it don't we? But we get along all right. . . . We like it here don't we Joe? He likes mending watches. . . . He likes mending them, it gets on my nerves. . . .'

Mr and Mrs Sewell live in a small terraced house. They are unemployed and share the shopping. They no longer meet people from the hostel in which they lived and their social worker is concerned about their overdependence on her. Mrs Sewell said:

'I do the cooking in the kitchen and the washing . . . and cleaning and all that . . . I learned in a flat in the hostel. . . .'

Mr Sewell said:

*'We go out shopping . . . I love her you know. She spoils me. She brought me
these boots and this watch. Boots for the snow. . . .'*

Miss Greaves is soon to marry Mr Harlow, a man she has been living with since
her mother died. They share all of the household tasks. They have few contacts
with people other than their families. He gave up his place at the ATC as she did
not like his daily absence. She said:

*I spoils him . . . I bought him a new suit and then I gives him money for spending
money, then I buys him cigs . . . then if he's short I gives him money. . . . I never
used to share you know, I used to keep it to meself. I didn't share . . . I know now I
have to now as I'm getting married . . . I follows him . . . I gets terrified in case he
might be with somebody else and leave me on me own again you know. . . .
[Friends at her former place of work] they keep saying to me . . . if he likes you,
he'll not go. I said, "But I don't trust him." . . . Nobody [visits] really, I falls out
with them me, that's why I don't have nobody me because I falls out with them . . .
I'm cruel, I'm cruel at times, and then I makes friends . . . but I always falls out
with them.'*

These insights into people's close relationships demonstrate that the companionship of a partner is valued and important. It seems possible that the preparation
of adults for independent living blurs the traditional male and female household
roles. It was evident that with the exception of Mr Sewell, all the men I met
involved themselves in routine household tasks. Unemployment may also play a
part in involving male partners in the running of households. However, the
Central Statistical Office (1983) shows that a smaller number of males than
females involve themselves in household tasks. While having a partner is not a
guarantee against loneliness and isolation, with the exception of one couple, social
workers were very positive about their married and cohabiting clients' achievements.

Only one man has the custody of his child. Mr Taylor's daughter is six, and since
his wife left him he has kept a full-time job and immersed himself in his daughter's
upbringing. With the assistance of a home help and a home carer (known as Aunty
Rita), a social worker, and a foster mother who looks after his daughter until Mr
Taylor gets home from work, Mr Taylor's accomplishments are a tremendous
source of pride to his social services department.

Two women have had children but no longer have the custody of them. This
includes Mrs Ellis who looked after her children until they went to school, at which
time her husband left her and he and his new partner acquired custody.

*'I see my children at my sister in law's. Since the divorce I've told my husband, if I
go round to our home, it was in my name, I'll beat the woman that broke us up.
My husband had a child by her when she was only thirteen. He was taken to
courts but he still has the children. Most weekends I see the children. When I was*

married I stayed in the house. My husband was always out with his cousin. I was always in with the children. He'd never take me out. When I was in I sometimes had as many as ten [epileptic] fits a day. It was hard. . . .'

Miss Jordan looked after her daughter for seven months, unsupported before she was fostered. She makes infrequent visits to see her daughter and the experience has become especially difficult since her daughter reached adolescence. Miss Jordan's social worker always accompanies her and chats to the daughter more comfortably than her client can. The social worker is concerned that Miss Jordan is distressed by the visits, but as her client does not want them to cease, dealing with these is a feature of the support. During one visit Miss Jordan's daughter was overheard as she said to her foster mother, 'I wish they'd go. I don't like Marjorie, she's thick.' As a result of this, the social worker does the talking and Miss Jordan, having primed her social worker with questions beforehand, remains silent.

Parenthood for one woman in her early teens resulted in incarceration in a hospital for people with mental handicap. The extent of contact she had with her family during her many years of institutionalisation is unknown. At 79 she is the oldest person in the study. She has been living in a co-residency with two other women for three years. It is noteworthy that in addition to help from her social worker, this woman is also supported by her son and his family. She delights in her lately endowed independence but is somewhat confused by her status:

'Me son comes. I have a son. He's got a son married and the other one works. I'm not a grandmother yet. Who'd make me a grandmother? I don't think anybody would. Oh yes, I am a grandmother.'

CO-RESIDENTS

In total, 38 people live with two or more people who are unrelated to them. This includes a woman who has a bedsit in a block of bedsits for people who are elderly; two men who live with a young family with no handicapped members; and in one area, three women and two men who live in group homes with people described as mentally ill. The social contact, mutual help and difficulties that arise from living with others is evidenced from the following quotations:

One of two women sharing a flat said of their lives:

'In social life I only bother with Sarah actually. . . . If Sarah does one meal then I wash up, and if I do one meal Sarah washes up. We do it like that. We're fair with one another, we don't let one do all the lot because it's teamwork, two together. . . . That's what a flat means, it's two working. . . . We can't live on our own but Sarah and I can live together. I couldn't cope on me own.'

These women explained that they give each other '*a break*' at weekends by visiting their families. This ensures that they do not, '*get on top of each other*'.

A woman sharing a flat with a woman much younger than herself said:

'*It's all right, we get on very well, except that she goes out a lot because of her training [running]. I give out to her, I told her off. She keeps going out and leaving me on me own.*'

A man who shares with another man he met in the hostel is also somewhat disillusioned with his co-resident:

'*In flat with Peter. He doesn't work. He used to go to hostel. He used to work here before. He does nothing now. He does shopping. Saturday morning I go.*'

A woman who shares a house with two other women who are described as mentally ill, outlined their household routine for cleaning and washing.

'*We helps one another and works together. I do me own room and things. I wash me own things. I don't use the machine, I don't know how to use it. Only Madeline knows how to use it. She does the sheets and things like that.*'

This woman is very talkative and, in contrast, her co-residents are mostly silent. For their sakes, her social worker encourages her to stay with her family each weekend.

Four women have lived in their own home for eleven years. They all met in a hospital for people with mental handicap, and as they are very able people their roles frequently blurred between those of patients and nursing assistants. They have mutual friends many of whom are from the hospital. Interestingly, however, and in contrast to the majority of the people I met, their visitors do not have a mental handicap. One woman described their association with friends:

'*Our friends come to see us . . . like the nurses who used to be at the hospital, they help us. They come to see us, Nurse Watkins and Sister Wilkinson come and see us. They used to work with us on B7, the babies ward. And Sister Baily. Dave [social worker] comes down too, and Miss Curran, she used to be a Guide leader. She used to have us in the Guides when we were small. On Wednesday and Sunday she still comes.*'

This group's household tasks are shared and the housework is a routine:

'*Liz cleans on Friday, polishing and that and Dorothy does the dusting. I scrubbed the carpet today with some stuff and I scrubbed the two carpets upstairs on Tuesday. Sally cooks every night and when she goes to pottery, Dorothy does it.*'

In contrast to this household, a group of four men lead lives largely independent of one another. The views of two men in this household are presented:

> 'We do the cleaning between us. . . . We help with the cleaning . . . we do our own washing and our own ironing. Sometimes we go out, watch telly. We go out by ourselves. I said, "Why don't we go out one night together, have a drink together?" I don't know . . . I've been to the pub with Dave [co-resident], he's all right with me . . . sometimes Joseph [co-resident] stays in.'
> 'I'd like to move, or live on me own me . . . I wash me own clothes, I don't wash anybody elses. If they don't wash theirs, that's too bad. It's not fair on the rest of them. . . . We do our own tea and that. . . . They just leave their plates, I always wash mine.'

A similar pattern emerges in another group home for four men:

> 'We do the cleaning when it needs it. Chris does it most because he's in. We do it as well sometimes. . . . We got a washing machine and we use that. We do our own.'

A woman living in a bedsit in a block of bedsits for people who are elderly had the following observations to make about her living arrangement:

> 'There is a place where they all communicate, I never go down. Sometimes there's people in, looking at magazines and reading, nothing like, great exciting. But now, sometimes we have like "dos" [functions] there. Not long since we had an Christmas Fayre here. I were invited to come along and that and I really enjoyed it . . . you know what I mean, all gathered together and a few outsiders come in and that were quite nice really. You know what I mean, meeting different people . . . [I] might have a little talk on the corridor you came down. I like the old lady. She's a mother of eight what lives facing me at number 28.'

One of two men living with no handicapped member family said:

> 'I've been here a bit now. I was here last year, the first year. . . . It's all right here, Susan's all right and Tom. . . . It's all right here. It's the outside problems what does it.'

Given that only 13 people talked of their living situation in negative terms and only nine people expressed a desire to change this, it appears that people are mostly satisfied with their living arrangements.

FAMILIES

Families have always had an important role in the care of their members with mental handicap and they remain the major care-takers in this country. Arguably the families who involve themselves in the lives of people in this study did not anticipate that the populations of hospitals and hostels would ever be encouraged to decline. Studies report that families are sceptical of community alternatives to institutions. They believed that they offered a permanent home (Payne, 1976; Meyer, 1980).

This section touches on a range of experiences and indicates some of the difficulties experienced by some people in relation to their families. Although we know that families applaud deinstitutionalisation, normalisation and integration in the abstract, they resist this for their sons/daughters/brothers/sisters (Card, 1983; Ferrara, 1979). As Byrne and Cunningham (1985) observe, 'These views are perhaps explicable when one considers parents' factually based perception that community attitudes towards mentally handicapped people are relatively negative' (p. 856).

An important study by Latib, Conroy and Hess (1984) examined the impact on families before and after their relatives with mental handicap moved from large institutions to small community-based facilities. With reservations regarding the representativeness of the sample, the most striking result was the overwhelmingly positive change of attitude among families – in other words, they came to see the advantages of life outside large institutions for their own relatives. Bearing this in mind, this chapter moves on to look at people's association with their families.

Social workers estimated that some 33 people have regular contact with their families, 23 have intermittent contact and 22 people have no contact at all. One social worker did not know about his client's contact and this information was missing for nine people. Given the age range of the study population (from 22 to 79 years), contact with families generally refers to contact with siblings and their families rather than with parents.

The circumstances of five people merit mention as they are different. One man, described in Chapter 3, lives with and looks after his elderly father who is physically handicapped. Two sisters who spent many years together in a hospital for people with mental handicap currently share a home. Similarly, two brothers live together and have done so for many years. They are also described in Chapter 3.

Some of the younger people I met referred to their visits to their families:

'*Me mum and dad live near. They come occasionally. I always go at weekends.*'

'*Sometimes me mum and dad come. I went there on Sunday. Sometimes I go during the week.*'

'*My sisters come a lot and I go to my parents. I see my family a lot.*'

Two people spoke angrily of their parents:

> *'Fourteen bloody years since I last seen my mam. She couldn't care less. I just get down half the time, get cheesed off, fed up.'*

> *'I've been very hurt. I haven't had a very good life with me parents. . . . If me dad sees me in the pub he says, "What the bloody hell are you doing here?" and he sends me out. He doesn't like me going in pubs. Now look at me, I'm 27 and they still treat me like a two-year-old. I can't make it out at all.'*

Of the sibling relationship, Powell and Ogle (1985) observe:

> Siblings play a critical role in our lives. Brothers and sisters know us like no one else. They have been with us during the good times and the bad. Siblings constitute our first social network, and their early influence affects us throughout our lives. Our sibling relationships are typically the longest relationship we will have in life. (p. xiii)

Siblings are closely involved in the lives of eleven people in total; in other words, they visit and/or are visited regularly and maintain contact with their brother's/sister's social worker. One way of approaching the relationships people have with their siblings is to examine a range of people's descriptions of these. In spite of people's independence in terms of their living arrangements, it will be seen that some siblings do have expectations of their handicapped brothers and sisters that cannot be realised. This is powerfully illustrated by a man who lives alone:

> *'I like to come home, have me telly on and done me hobbies like that, and me brother doesn't approve of all that. Me brother says I should go in the garden [gardening]. . . . I'm not very keen on it. This house is rented . . . [the rent] I give to me brother and he takes it to the place and he pays it . . . without him I'd be lost. . . . See me brother's always looked after me mum and he's looked after the family . . . he used to look after me and we used to have terrible rows . . . He's just the opposite to what I am. He rows with everybody. . . . Trouble is, he doesn't like the way I eat. I can't help it. I just like chips you see. Trouble is it makes me fat and I can't get into me clothes properly and he gets upset about that. . . . I just like to come in and enjoy meself doing pictures. He doesn't approve of that. . . . Me sister's coming this Sunday, I give me washing to her. . . . They phone up, see how I'm getting on, see if I'm all right. . . . I don't have any friends at all. Only friends I have is me brother.*

This man's position is shared to a lesser extent by that of a woman who lives with her boyfriend. She said of her sister, *'Sometimes she interferes but I think she's only doing it, thinking of me like, you know.'* Another man who is regularly visited by his brother was critical and despondent when talking about his brother:

'Now and again he comes down on a Saturday to see me. I've not never been [to his house]. He doesn't like me most of the time. I don't know why because I am his flesh and blood when all's said and done. . . . He wanted me put away he did. . . .'

One woman has ceased to see her family as a result of her changed living circumstances and dislike of their expectations:

'My sister doesn't come. None of my family come. . . . I've got a twin sister and older sister and she's finished with me altogether since I moved in here, because I was living with her at the time. . . . I only get criticised when I go. She criticises me and it upsets me. She doesn't like Alan and Alan don't like her. . . . She said, "You're no sister of mine. Where's your glasses? You look a state, you look ill, you look a tramp." Then she just walked away.'

In the main, shared activities with families include preparing and sharing meals, going shopping, going drinking and going on day excursions. One woman has decorated her elderly mother's flat. One man and his sister regularly visit children's homes as they were brought up in one and they remember what it was like not having any visitors. This appeared to be the most satisfying sibling relationship that was described. Two social workers expressed concern that their clients are too generously disposed towards their siblings and regularly give them money from their meagre incomes. Another social worker believes that his client is sexually abused by her brother, but he has no evidence to support this. He also believes that she has become a prostitute.

Reading letters and helping people to sort out their money are frequent points of contact with siblings. One woman described her routine:

'What I generally do, I generally leave me money with me sister-in-law. I generally take it every week and she sorts me money out for me. And like, if a bill comes, I generally take it to me sister-in-law's.'

During the course of the study I met one person's sibling. He interpreted his brothers' speech and signing as these are so idiosyncratic. He is concerned about his brother's drinking problem and has reservations about his ability to manage independently:

[Tapping his forehead] 'I've had it up to here. I preferred it when he was in the hostel. He drinks his money and he's round at our place for meals. I've had him all me life.'

Regardless of the anguished relationships some people have with their families, the interviews suggested that 48 people are in the habit of visiting their families regularly and 39 are visited by them. The frequency of visits to and by families is not known. This information was not sought in the interview because of the difficulties many people experience regarding time, dates and frequency (see Flynn, 1986(b)).

'*Go at Christmas as well as Mondays. They take me home night time.*'

'*When it's fine I go to me sister's in Dene Road.*'

'*I see my family when they come and me other brother comes.*'

'*I see Eveline my sister. She lives in hostel. She used to live at hospital, my sister. I don't smoke, me. She does, I don't.*

Some people expressed regret at the absence of contact with their families and recalled their bereavements:

'*My mum lives in Manchester. I don't see her. I got brothers and I don't see them much. I wish I did see them more.*'

'*I've got an Aunty in Wiltshire and she's 94. . . . Then I've got a brother but he doesn't bother with me.*'

'*Me mum died just before last Christmas. I used to go round there every day and help her cook. She's dead now though and that really upset me mostly. I've got no parents now. I've got a dad but I don't know where he is. I've got sisters of course but I never bother with them. They don't bother with me so I don't bother with them.*'

NEIGHBOURS

In order to extend the impression of the social milieu in which different people live, contact with neighbours was a topic addressed in interviews. A stereotype of people of northern England is that of friendliness and openness with plenty of conversations over the garden fence. While this image is not entirely sustained by the information gathered, it is clear that some people enjoy the association they have with neighbours.

Social workers estimated that 38 people have regular contact with their neighbours, 32 have intermittent contact and seven have no contact. Five social workers did not know about their clients' contact with neighbours and this information was missing for six people.

It is noteworthy that two households I visited enjoy frequent association, as they had all lived in the same hostel and are neighbours. Two women live next door to three men and they are happy with the close contact that their proximity permits. In total 59 people described their neighbours in terms of exchanging greetings; 25 people visit their neighbours and 30 people are visited by their neighbours.

I was aware of neighbourliness in three interviews in particular. When I arrived at one man's flat, he and his elderly neighbour were struggling to unblock his sink. She had offered to help when he went to her for advice. When the sink was unblocked they congratulated each other and arranged to meet later for a cup of tea. It emerged that when this man is absent from his flat, his neighbour looks after his dog and many houseplants. In turn, he looks after his neighbour's flat when she is away. Following an interview with an elderly woman, a neighbour arrived and explained that this was the evening that pensioners went to town as some stores were opening just for people who were elderly [prior to Christmas]. Apologising to me she said, 'Come on Sylvie, we don't want to miss our pensioners' rights.' Finally, when I arrived at another woman's flat, I was introduced to a woman referred to as 'Aunty'. Aunty was leaving and before she did so the two women embraced and kissed each other. The woman later explained that this person was not really her aunty, but *'a good friend, like an aunty'* who lived in the same block of flats. It is noteworthy that these three people live alone.

The following quotations suggest the types of association that people have with their neighbours. A man who lives alone said:

'They're all right. There's me mates down the road. I've been here a long while so they know me. The woman next door gets on at me sometimes, but they're OK. Not like the next street, they don't look at you down there.'

A woman who lives alone said:

'They're all nice. They all talk to me and everything . . . They're all old people, I'm the youngest one out of all of them. I'm 54 this year.'

Another woman living by herself said:

'I got good neighbours up here. . . . I know Mrs what's her name, Mrs Briggs and Clare, the lady with the bad leg. There's quite a few I know. The lady with the glasses on, we talk to one another, "How do Lizzie, haven't seen you for ages." "Haven't seen you. . . ." There's old people on this floor you see . . . we talk to one another and she takes in milk for me when I'm at work. . . .'

A woman living with a partner said:

'They're smashing. She's all right next door. She spoke to me this morning next door. I told her "I'm going out" and she said "I'm going in . . . weather seems a bit better" and I said "Yes, about time!" She said "Have a nice time."'

Another woman living with her partner said:

'Very nice. Mrs Blake is next door. I generally go in there and have a natter with her.'

A man living with his partner said:

> '*They're nice. We don't know them that well but we get on all right with them. They're friendly.*'

A woman who lives with her female friend said of their neighbours:

> *They're lovely. They don't bother us and we don't bother them. They've got an idea where we come from but you never hear me and Sarah falling out or crying. . . . The neighbours are so nice they even look after the flat, I'm not kidding you . . . they don't half look after me and Sarah. . . . When I first moved in I told him we was his new neighbours and he carried boxes up for me.*'

A couple of issues are touched on in the preceding quotations that concern other people in the study. One is unwelcome interference by neighbours and the other, location in flats that are for elderly people. In the interviews some 23 people complained about their neighbours and 12 people recollected complaints that had been made.

A man who lives alone said:

> '*They don't like me very much. I've had some rows you know. They don't like my tapes and records.*'

A man who lives with three male friends said of his neighbours:

> '*It's all right but the neighbours are always on at us.*'

A single woman elaborated about the difficulty she has experienced with her neighbours and the consequences of this for her life:

> '*Some of the old ladies you know that live upstairs, they don't like anyone making a lot of noise . . . they like people to be very quiet in the flat, and if you're not . . . they don't tell you they go and tell somebody else you know. Like they go down to the hostel and tell Mrs Benyon like you're making a noise . . . and she said next time she won't complain to Mrs Benyon, she'll complain to the rent office. . . . So when I told Billy [boyfriend], I don't know whether he took the hump . . . but he stopped coming so often after that you know. Because she says to me "When I see your boyfriend, I'll tell him to see if he can't be a bit quieter in the flat."*'

A young couple are very disappointed to be living in a flat in a block mostly for elderly people:

> '*At the moment we don't get enough sleep because of the one above us complaining all the time. She bangs on the ceiling with a stick to wake us up. . . . There's*

only one person round here that speaks to us. A woman above with a baby. What they've done is put us in these flats with old people. There's more old people living here and what they should have done is put us with younger people, because we're only young ourselves.'

One couple stand out in respect of their association with their neighbours. They live in a notoriously poor area and have endured many hardships. They have unrealistic expectations regarding the role of their neighbours:

'I've got no food in today, nothing in. I'm starving. The neighbours won't help me, they're nasty. . . . Mind you I keep to meself round here mind you. I don't like to get involved with the neighbours. They're very good with the dog, they're good with Spot, but they won't feed me an' him you see. We're starving. . . .'

A consideration of neighbours is inadequate without some reference to neighbourhoods. It should be recalled that some 22 people live in 'hard to let' housing, that is in tenancies and/or areas that are undesirable. Fourteen people talked of their fear of neighbours and young children and described their anxieties about leaving their homes. While this issue is addressed in Chapter 5, one man's experiences are reported because they are so exceptional. His concerns about the safety of his flat have resulted in closer contact with his neighbour:

'I don't know the people on the left but the Irishman next door's got a dog and it barks so much it scares people off and keeps my flat safe. I generally go in when I get back from my sister's. We have a chat then I go off to bed.'

In the interviews, nine people talked of their desire to have different neighbours, such was their dislike of them. The overall picture, however, suggests that people have friendly relations with neighbours.

SUMMARY

There are difficulties in gathering valid data on people's relationships and social activities, particularly in a study that can only give a snapshot impression of people's lives at one point in time. Often people referred to their social workers as friends. Most people have regular contact with individuals who may be described as friends.

In total, 26 people live alone, 37 live with one other person and 25 live with two or more than two others. Mostly people's living arrangements reflect their active preferences. They are not typical, however, when compared with the population of the United Kingdom – in other words, they are less likely to be living in families and to have their own families.

Some people who live alone are lonely and isolated, others have developed friendships with people from the hospitals and/or hostels in which they lived, and with people in their localities. There are three married couples in the study population and six couples are living together. The companionship of partners is valued and important; thirty-eight people live with one or more other persons who are unrelated to them, and thirteen people talked of their living arrangements in negative terms.

Social workers estimated that 33 people have regular contact with their families and 23 have intermittent contact. Siblings are closely involved with the lives of eleven people in total. Social workers estimate that 38 people have regular contact with their neighbours but not everybody enjoys association with them. What is clear is that the social integration of people with mental handicap and living in their own homes cannot be assumed.

7

The Formal Support of People Living in Their Own Homes

In recent years we have come to realise that adults with mental handicap can live in their own homes, provided they have a broad range of services available to meet their needs. It will have been gathered from the preceding chapters that the people I met varied considerably in terms of their circumstances, abilities and their needs. This chapter explores the support provided by professionals in order to help people to maintain their independence.

The chapter begins by looking at the formal support services which are available to people, outlining the specific tasks that social services and community mental handicap team (CMHT) personnel are engaged in. The extent to which support corresponds to people's needs is explored. Next, the frequency of contact with support personnel is examined. People's views about their support personnel follow, and the extent to which social workers are a part of their clients' social networks and frequently fulfil the function of friends is discussed. Social workers' objectives for their clients are outlined and social workers' ratings of their clients' placements are presented. Lastly, the contact people have with other agencies is described.

THE TASKS OF SUPPORT PERSONNEL

Two of the areas in which I worked are served by community mental handicap teams and the remaining four by specialist and non-specialist social workers. Although the distinction between these sources of support was not investigated, informally it did not appear that people were in receipt of vastly different services.

Support is concerned with helping people to live in their own homes. If we are to try to tackle some of the difficulties of supporting people living independently, it is necessary to be a good deal more precise about what it is, and what in fact are the tasks being carried out by support personnel. Support was examined by looking at the type of help that social workers provide and describe in case records. This help varies from shopping with people to helping people to arrange their holidays. For people to achieve independent living, social workers' attention is paid to people's skills and the extent to which these are wanting. The provision of services is then directed at meeting people's different levels of competence and circumstances.

The areas for which support is available have been sorted into the following categories: money; health and hygiene; home and household management; family and interpersonal issues; daily occupation and leisure. In Chapter 2 reference was made to the way in which the information gathered was analysed. Initially eleven areas of interest were identified and within these areas, indices were developed. The association between indices was examined using Pearson Product Moment Correlations. The creation of indices made it possible to look at the characteristics of the people who are receiving support in respect of these different categories. Only those correlations which were significant at the 5 per cent level or less are described in this chapter. The detailed results of the correlations appear in Appendix 1.

ASSISTANCE WITH MONEY

The types of support people receive in respect of money management and the numbers in receipt of these are presented in Table 7.1. Social workers act on

Table 7.1 *Assistance with money matters*

Type of support	Number receiving this	Missing
Liaising with DHSS, explaining procedures and assisting with form completion	71	–
Monitoring payment of money for bills or rent	48	4
Arranging direct payment of gas, electricity or rent	43	7
Contacting charities for money	15	3

behalf of 71 people for purposes of liaising with the DHSS, explaining procedures and assisting with the completion of forms. In part this reflects people's low level of literacy. It has long been a source of concern that the literature and forms produced by the DHSS are difficult to follow. Over half of the people in this study have the payment of money for bills and rent monitored by their social workers. Naturally the type of help people receive varies according to the individuals concerned. Two elderly men who have lived in their own home for five years are visited at the end of each week by their social worker. He checks that his clients have put the necessary sums of money for bills in the requisite envelopes. On the occasions that the social worker has attempted to withdraw from this monitoring role, his clients have fallen into debt and are unable to account for their spending. This is one way of ensuring that debts do not mount up and it works for these two men.

A further example of assistance with money management is provided by a man who lives by himself. His case record is full of demands for the payment of bills spanning some five years. The only way that this man's social worker could ensure that her client would remain out of debt was to engage the services of the reception staff in the social services department. Each morning, from Monday to Friday, he goes to the social services and is given £3 by the reception staff.

The determination of social workers to ensure that their clients do not get behind with the payment of bills merits some comment. Ultimately debts come to their attention and require swift action if a person's gas or electricity is not to be cut off, for example. It will be recalled from Chapter 4 that these people experience difficulty in budgeting, and from Chapter 5, that people do not have large sums of money at their disposal, hence the fifteen applications to charities for money. The consequences of paying off debts over long periods are that sums of money are regularly subtracted from people's already limited incomes, leaving some with barely sufficient to survive. Invariably this results in dissatisfaction. It is highly likely that further debts will occur; social and leisure activities have to be curtailed; people are not able to buy clothes or things for their homes; they may become dependent upon charity; and they live at a subsistence level. Loneliness and depression are almost inevitable consequences.

A positive picture emerges when the characteristics of the people receiving support in money matters is considered. Help with the payment of bills and managing finances is more likely to be given to people who: have expressed dissatisfaction with their money management; have, or have had debts; are poor at managing money; receive benefits rather than a wage; and are poor at decision-making.

ASSISTANCE WITH HEALTH AND PERSONAL HYGIENE

Table 7.2 shows that social workers are especially active in the role of liaising with general practitioners/hospitals and dentists. Social workers tackle deterioration in health and personal hygiene for 30 people and a small number engage in direct health intervention. Deterioration in health partly relates to the advancing age of this population. The type of help people receive largely consists of sorting out tablets, often ensuring that someone has a week's supply to hand in order to minimise confusion. One social worker makes regular checks on her client's medication. Her client takes many tablets in addition to the contraceptive pill. Almost by chance the social worker found out that her client had been taking all her months' supply of pills at the beginning of the month. This prompted the

Table 7.2 *Assistance with health and personal hygiene*

Support	Number receiving this	Missing
Liaising with general practitioner/hospital and dentist	43	4
Tackling deterioration in health and hygiene	30	3
Direct health intervention	10	–

weekly checks on medication. It will be recalled from Chapter 4 that a number of people have weight problems. Two social workers have grasped this particular nettle by dieting with their clients. They monitor each other's weight loss and have low calorie lunches together.

In the table there are 30 people recorded as requiring reminders to bath and change their clothes (this information is missing for three people). In respect of personal hygiene, mostly social workers recorded explicit reminders to their clients regarding the necessity of frequently changing clothes and washing.

Support with health and hygiene is more likely to be given to people who: have medical problems and who need reminders to keep clean; have poor self care skills; and have communication problems.

ASSISTANCE WITH HOME AND HOUSEHOLD

Given that almost everybody lives in rented property, it is not surprising that social workers liaise with housing agencies on behalf of so many people (Table 7.3). Most social workers deal with the correspondence and arrangements for paying rent and they are involved in contacting housing agencies if repair work is necessary. Social workers are also involved in moving people from particular houses and/or areas.

Table 7.3 *Assistance with home and household*

Support	Number receiving this	Missing
Liaising with housing department and housing agencies	67	3
Monitoring cleanliness of home	61	3
Prompting the use of domestic skills	57	5
Arranging connection of essential supplies	54	4
Teaching self-help skills	47	4
Assisting with household tasks	46	4
Shopping with client	41	5

After this, the most frequently cited occupation of social workers is monitoring the cleanliness of people's homes; 23 people are recorded as experiencing difficulty in keeping their homes clean (with information missing for one person). Deterioration in the cleanliness of people's homes is met with varied responses from support personnel: some social workers help their clients to clean their homes; and/or help to establish a routine; and/or visit on the days that they know their clients will be cleaning. For some people, this has resulted in an extension of the support they receive. Fifteen, mostly elderly people, are in receipt of the additional services of home helps who do practical and domestic tasks such as cleaning. The exception is one man who has a full-time job and has the custody of his young daughter. He has a home help to assist with the cleaning and preparation of the evening meal. Table 7.3 shows that 57 people receive prompts to use their domestic skills; in other words, without support personnel nudging and encouraging people to use their skills, some tasks would not be accomplished.

In total 47 people are being taught self-help skills by support personnel. This finding merits some consideration. Social workers are not trained teachers, and yet developing people's skills is one of the multiplicity of tasks in which they are involved to enable people to continue living in their own homes. It will be recalled from Chapter 4 that only seventeen people attend ATCs. An even larger number used to attend but opted to retire or leave for reasons that included inadequate payment and not having adult status acknowledged. If people do not wish to attend ATCs then one solution is the picture that emerges from this study: social workers may assume the teaching role. The appropriateness of this is debatable.

The people who receive support regarding their homes are those who: are dissatisfied with their homes; live in poor quality homes; and live in flats rather than houses. While this confirms the pleasing picture of a responsive service, it is noteworthy that housing is an area over which social services personnel have only modest control. It will be recalled from Chapter 5 that people cannot expect to be placed in the most desirable residential areas and that over half of the population reside in flats. Social services personnel are supporting people who do not like their current homes and/or neighbourhoods. In a snapshot study that is looking at people's circumstances at one point in time, it is not possible to establish the overall effectiveness of support in this area. It should be pointed out, however, that problems with a tenancy, victimisation, and a preference to live elsewhere/ with somebody else, all constituted reasons for moving people to another tenancy. This suggests that, ultimately, people do move if they wish to do so.

ASSISTANCE WITH INTERPERSONAL ISSUES

In this area, counselling in respect of interpersonal issues is the most frequently cited occupation of social workers. As 62 people in this study live with one or more persons, invariably difficulties in relationships arise from time to time. Social workers may be summoned specifically to deal with problems of this nature. A number of social workers spoke of their knowledge of dominant people in particular households and their commitment to ensure that this did not result in unpleasantness for other members of the household. Difficulties with neighbours and youngsters affect a number of people's lives and some social workers help their clients to see ways of overcoming these. One extremely shy woman asked her social worker for help in overcoming her shyness. Over a number of weeks she and her partner worked through a programme developed with their social worker. This has enabled her to talk to people with more comfort than before.

Table 7.4 shows that social workers are in touch with the family members of 45 people. Much of this activity is of a reassuring nature. Because of the age range of the people in this study, the contact that people have is largely with siblings. Social workers acknowledge the concerns of family members and remind families that people are not being deserted. Some social workers also maintain contact with the families who do not want any association with their handicapped member. This contact is largely for information purposes, but it is also hoped that interest in the handicapped person will reawaken.

Table 7.4   *Assistance with family and interpersonal issues*

Support	Number receiving this	Missing
Counselling in respect of interpersonal issues	55	10
Contact with family members	45	3
Helping to establish the social network of the client	25	13
Discussions with the client re sex and/or contraception	21	18

Social workers are working on behalf of 25 people to help to establish their social networks. This reflects the fact that not everybody is blessed with friendships, and that for some people, contacts with non mentally handicapped people are more valued than contacts with people with mental handicap.

Six people are married and a further twelve people live with their partners. Some of the people in partnerships have been sterilised, although the extent to which this reflects their preferences is not known. One social worker who was unable to accompany her client for his appointment to have a vasectomy, sent her son in her place. It was clear that the social workers who were involved in discussions with their clients regarding sex and/or contraception experienced no discomfort with either the topics or the need to be extremely explicit. For example, following vasectomy operations, two men were required to take samples of semen to the hospital. Both made the error of taking urine samples and their social workers had to make it clear just what was required.

Support in the interpersonal sphere is more likely to be given to people who: have few relationships; are dissatisfied with their limited social lives; and are poor at handling relationships. Thus the evidence of a responsive and supportive service continues to be confirmed.

ASSISTANCE WITH DAILY AND LEISURE ACTIVITIES

In Chapter 4 it was shown that 44 people have unstructured daily lives in so far as they are retired or unemployed and not seeking work. A consideration of social workers' activities in respect of their clients' daily activities puts this into context. It will be seen from Table 7.5 that social workers encourage 39 people to engage in

Table 7.5 *Assistance with daily and leisure activities*

Support	Number receiving this	Missing
Encouraging daily activity	39	1
Liaising with place of daily occupation	30	–
Arranging day service/courses	16	2
Assisting with job search	9	2
Arranging provision of bus pass	58	5
Encouraging leisure activities	49	8
Arranging holiday	39	8
Arranging leisure-oriented classes	19	11

some form of activity and some 30 social workers liaise with the place of their clients' daily activities. For example, one man who works shifts, meets his social worker for lunch at his place of work. As he is unable to read, the arrangement is made through a colleague.

Ensuring mobility is a further occupation of social workers. Free bus passes are available to people in the North-West who are disabled, and at the time of the study social workers arranged the provision of these. Mindful of the large number of retired and unemployed people, reference to Table 7.5 indicates that 49 social workers encourage their clients to pursue leisure interests. This might take the form of encouraging people to join local clubs, participate in activities outside the home and/or use bus passes to go on day trips. One social worker whose client is an extremely keen and able gardener, encouraged him to join a local horticultural society. Her father is also a member and he arranged to give this man a lift for the first couple of weeks and to introduce him to other members.

In terms of the effectiveness of this support, the people who are most likely to receive assistance with their daily activities are people who have a structured day. In respect of leisure, the people who are most likely to receive help in this area are those who: are dissatisfied with their leisure; and are receiving support regarding their daily activities. While it is clear that, in general, people have access to a supportive service, in terms of daily and leisure activities, social workers are more responsive to the needs of people who have structured days – those who are in open and sheltered employment, voluntary work and ATCs. It appears that the people who are retired or unemployed do not receive the same support as their counterparts with organised daily activities.

A SUMMARY OF SOCIAL WORKERS' ACTIVITIES

On the measure, information from social workers, the latter were requested to summarise their activities regarding their clients. The results of this summary are presented in Table 7.6, and corroborates the findings that it is in the area of managing finances, paying bills and handling medical problems that people require most help. There is no information missing from Table 7.6.

Table 7.6   *A summary of social workers' activities*

Activities	Number of social workers engaged in activities
Management of money	66
Monitoring health and hygiene	62
Management of home and household	61
Management of interpersonal issues	53
Management of leisure/free time/retirement/ holidays	48
Management of work/occupation issues	36
Contact with and support for client's family	35

CONTACT WITH CLIENTS

Social workers were requested to indicate how often they have contact with their clients. Table 7.7 shows that 46 people see and/or have telephone contact with

Table 7.7   *Social workers' contact with clients*

	> Once a week	Once a week	Once a fortnight	Once a month	< Once a month
Workers see/have 'phone contact	25	21	5	16	21
Clients visit SSD*	10	9	6	11	50
Workers visit clients' homes	16	23	4	20	25

* This information is missing for two people.

their clients once a week or more than once a week. Some ten people visit their social services department/community mental handicap team more than once a week, and sixteen people are visited by their social workers more than once a week.

PEOPLE'S VIEWS REGARDING SOCIAL WORKERS

This study pinpoints a heavy reliance on help from support personnel. The interviews indicated that 69 people regularly received help from the social services department/community mental handicap teams, sixteen people said that they had help when necessary and a further three said that they had no support. For eleven people, social workers are their only visitors and for a further nine people, social workers and siblings are their only visitors. These figures suggest much greater assistance from social services personnel than from such informal sources as families and friends. This picture is corroborated by Malin's (1983) investigation of six group homes and Atkinson's (1980) study of the lives of 50 former residents of a hospital. The majority of people are in regular contact with their social workers and the importance of the resulting relationships cannot be underestimated.

'Social worker sorts me money out. It's Susan.'

'Fran's taking me cat to the vet to be done. It has to be done for my benefit and the cat's. She's something to do with social services. I can't think what.'

'If I want for anything then I phone Peter up. If I want for anything urgent he'll come down in the car.'

'I go out on Saturdays and I buy in things that I can have in the week. When Peter comes on Monday he looks in the kitchen to see what there is. And Phil comes on Wednesdays. He does some of the cooking sometimes.'

'Bill comes on Tuesday morning. We don't do anything. We just weigh ourselves and just have a talk to see how I am . . . Bill was telling me last week that they've started doing art classes at the tech. and would I like to go. I said, "Well I wouldn't mind having a try."'

'We need some light bulbs putting in. Mary will help. There are some bricks coming out near the window. I told Mary about it.'

'Richard said to me, "Tell your brother we would not have you in a flat if you had not been capable of going in a flat." He said, "You're sensible Bernadette, You've got your faculties, you're sensible. Tell him not to worry."'

'Rachel comes every week. She chats and she sees how we're getting on. She's nice. Sometimes we go and see her at the social services. She got this flat for us. She said she thought we'd like it. It's warm and we like it.'

'When a bill comes we give it to June. She puts bulbs in for us when they go off, bulbs for lights. . . . Yes, I like June, I've made a friend of her.'

'Simon comes along and he'll say, "Is there anything we must know about?" He'll never miss. So I put things on that letter thing, he's like to come along and give me a bit of help with it. That's why they help because it means a great deal to me.'

'She bumps down when there's anything up. Something to do with the Housing, somebody not doing any work. We bring her down and we all have a chat about it. Find out why it's not going so well.'

'Frank is going to learn me how to use the washing machine when he's got time, 'cause I don't know how to use it you see. He showed May and Irene but I wasn't here you see.'

'I bought Josie a stick of rock when I went to Southport. I gave it to one of the social workers to give to her and she said she'd enjoyed it . . . she's been good to me.'

'See Steve's supposed to be our social worker, but it's been over two months since he was last up. I mean it's bloody annoying. We don't know where we're up to with them.'

'She's very nice only very small. She's very nice to talk to and things like that. She's been me social worker for quite a long time. She got me out of hospital when I'd been there for a long time.'

'I must tell Liz to give me sister a ring. . . . She's a nice person is Liz. She's like a mother to me. If I have any problems I have to tell her or explain to her.'

'I'm going to Wales with Bill. It's very nice. We do lots of walking.'

'I've not been well. Like when Tony left me I was really depressed. I cried me eyes out. . . . I went to his office and oh, I cried. I got him a card for leaving, "Congratulations on your new job." I must write to him.'

'I wish I could have children, me. I wish somebody could have got me one. And do you know what Sheila said? Oh, she was a laugh, she said, "I'll ask me husband and see what he can do for you." I had to laugh. I said "At his age, you must be joking."'

These observations about people's social workers highlight a number of issues. Nearly everybody is on first-name terms with their social worker, and almost half of the study population have their social workers' home telephone numbers. It seems likely that the ingenuousness of these people has some bearing on the style of relationships I observed and heard about. Notions of professional distance are perhaps dissipated with tasks that span day trips to buy clothes, to explaining what sort of samples are required by hospitals.

From the preceding sections and chapters it appears that social workers are involved in areas of people's lives that are often reserved for friends such as meeting and talking about family members, talking and advising about relationships, diets and activities. In the above quotations, people's perceptions of their social workers included, 'a friend', and 'a mother'. Some people have had the same social worker for many years. Many people spoke with great affection and warmth of their social workers and inevitably this was often reciprocated. One social worker spoke of her role in helping people in one group home to patch up their interpersonal difficulties. She said 'After talking about the difficulties of getting on, we repair it, give each other a hug and carry on, trying to be sensitive to each other.'

There was a lot of evidence of unrecorded social work activity. For example, in a number of interviews people talked about their social workers coming for meals; meeting them in their local pub in the evenings; visiting and getting to know their social workers' families; and events such as birthdays being celebrated with social workers. Such informal contacts and association inevitably creates difficulties when the issue of continued support is considered. Criticisms did arise concerning support personnel and these largely concerned the desire for more contact. One couple had not had any visits from their social worker for the four months prior to my visit. They were bewildered by the apparent neglect and throughout the visit, were occasionally distracted by cars being parked locally in the hope that Frank, their social worker would arrive. I was asked to relate the following message to Frank:

'Tell him we've not seen him for ages. It's me birthday soon and is he coming and I've got a can of beer in the fridge waiting for him.'

This couple's level of competence in managing their own lives was such that they were being weaned off the support provided by their social worker. Although they were managing, they were ill-prepared for their social worker's reduction of visits.

One couple demonstrated their attachment to their social worker by moving to the locality to which she had transferred. The couple gave up a desirable council tenancy in exchange for a 'hard to let' tenancy in a very depressed area. The social worker was horrified when the couple explained that they had moved so that she could remain their social worker.

Social workers are expensive friends and the withdrawal of support is not compatible with the way in which their clients see them. They spend time with their clients in different settings; they are familiar with their clients' lives and circumstances; they are accustomed to self-disclosure and this is often reciprocated. Some social workers are physically affectionate towards their clients, especially the older people. Although I did not explore social workers' perceptions of their role in respect of their clients, informally gathered evidence suggested that the friendships that the study population described when talking of their contacts with social services personnel are not unilateral. In the following section of this chapter it will be seen that a number of social workers regard the withdrawal of support as their objective for their clients. Once again, this points to the incompatibility with the way in which clients see their social workers.

Finally it should be pointed out that these social workers do not have unlimited access to their clients' homes. They do not go into their client's homes without acquiring permission beforehand. They are invited in and the help they offer is negotiated and frequently reviewed. Their clients' views are respected and attendance at ATCs, for example, is not enforced if people do not wish to go. In short, these people are treated as adults who can and do make decisions about their own lives.

SOCIAL WORKERS' OBJECTIVES FOR THEIR CLIENTS

Social workers were requested to specify their main objectives for their clients on the measure information from social workers. The responses to this were categorised and these are presented in Table 7.8. The table shows that 24 social workers cite as their main objective the need to maintain the independence/self-management of their clients in the community. Typical responses within this category are:

> to maintain existing lifestyle . . . to maintain open employment . . . to continue to live happily and successfully within the community . . . to maintain his present lifestyle, that is employment and independent living with improve-

Table 7.8 *Social workers' objectives for their clients*

Objective	Number of workers citing this
Maintain independence/self-management in community	24
Increase independence/self-management in community	17
Physical/psychological health related	10
Independence/self-management with support	9
Fulfilling relationship with partner/friends/family	8
Fulfilling work/day service/retirement activity	6
Improve home/material circumstances	6
Improve management of finances	4
Other	2

ments to his home conditions, that is decorating . . . . For her to continue in the group living situation and to have regular contact with her mother, brother and his family . . . to continue living in the community like any other person.'

Social workers indicated that they aimed to increase the independence/self-management of 17 people. The type of responses are as follows:

'becoming more independent . . . maximum independence within his capabilities . . . greater independence and a higher level of social skills. . . . Greater independence – he would like a flat of his own, possibly with girlfriend – job also . . . for client to do more for himself . . . to help him to be more able to manage his affairs without assistance . . . to become less dependent on professionals.'

Ten social workers cited physical/psychological health related objectives for their clients. Responses included: 'daytime activity and good health . . . to live a happy life . . . to keep himself and his home clean and tidy and get rehoused into more manageable accommodation . . . weight loss.'

Nine social workers cited independence/self-management with support as their main objective and typical responses included:

'self-management in the community with help with clothing from WRVS and grants for shoes . . . to be supported so that she be allowed to live as normal a life as is possible in the community . . . that he maintains his current level of competence in self-help skills with the available help of the non handicapped family who co-reside with him . . . to support them in the community . . . giving support to maintain as much stability as possible through a structured life style.'

As some of the examples of objectives have shown, a number of social workers did not limit themselves to one objective. Some social workers indicated that in addition to their main objective, they are working towards their clients having fulfilling relationships with partner, friends and family and fulfilling daily activities (see Flynn, 1985b, for an account of social workers' short-term objectives).

Overall it appears that social workers are committed to maintaining and improving their clients' circumstances. They are mindful also of the need to facilitate their clients' independence by means of increasing people's skills for self management. It can be seen, however, that in terms of their major preoccupation, the management of money, the improvement of this is regarded as an objective for only four people.

RATINGS OF SUCCESS

Social workers were requested to rate the success of their clients' placements on the measure, information from social workers. If they did not regard their clients as overly successful, they were asked to suggest the reasons for this. In total 61 people are described as 'successful', 22 people are described as 'moderately successful', and four are described as 'not successful'. One social worker indicated that she was unsure how to rate her client.

The reasons that social workers suggest are responsible for people's limited success are important to consider. They give some indication of the characteristics of the individuals and their environments that support personnel recognise as fundamental to people's management and independence. Consequently, the reasons for lack of success are quoted in full. The initial ones deal with the people and their characteristics and these are followed by reasons that concern people's environments past and present.

- His personality and overdependence on professionals – he tends not to plan a social life unless he has someone such as a social worker to go out with; the result is isolation. Also, personal neglect, untidiness and rubbish-hoarding appear an immature reaction to a lack of attention from professionals and his family. He had longstanding behaviour problems before he lived independently.
- Client is very shy and withdrawn, reluctant to attempt change even though the family is willing to support.
- He is resistant to change in habits, possibly due to his age. But there has been an improvement and an interest in home circumstances since I've known him, as well as his well-being.
- His health is not good. He is lonely but shy of people and of new acquaintances.
- He needs to become more of an individual.
- She has been institutionalised for most of her life and it's difficult for her to develop any kind of routine.
- There has been moderate success because of the lack of planning of the placement.
- The placement is 'successful', but he has got fed up of living as a group of four and now wants to live with just one other friend.
- Due to his working, more training should be given.
- She was employed in a kitchen enclave, but because of a relationship problem with another employee, walked out and refused to return. Since then she has been unemployed.
- Housing estate viewed as a dumping ground with no real community spirit. Isolation results from lack of ability to live with such a community, as she is an easy target for gangs that live on the estate.
- Because of problems with vandals, client is at risk [social worker noted this on behalf of two clients].
- She has lived at her present address for three months but this particular placement appears to be the most stable home background that she has experienced in the community to date.

In sum, these reasons highlight the importance of people: not relying entirely on professionals; being able to meet and get on with others; being interested in their home circumstances; and having routines. With reference to people's placements, these should: be planned; be stable, yet allowing people to move on if they wish; offer training; and be conscious of the consequences of location in less than benign neighbourhoods.

CONTACT WITH OTHER AGENCIES

In this section, the contact that people have with doctors (general practitioners), psychiatrists, housing agencies and the Department of Health and Social Security is explored. It will be recalled from Chapter 4 that a number of people have medical problems that bring them to the attention of health services. Social workers estimate that 25 people see their general practitioners regularly and 39 see them intermittently. Four social workers do not know about their clients' contact with general practitioners and the information is missing for a further six people. This degree of contact ties in with the variety of medical problems people have. Seven people in total are subject to periods of mental illness, and of these people three are seen regularly by a psychiatrist and two are seen intermittently. Ten people have regular contact with a nurse or health visitor and a further ten have intermittent contact. These people tend to be at the older end of the age range. (This information is missing for thirteen people.) The help that people receive spans dressing sores to advising about weight and diet.

It is noteworthy that one social worker was extremely disappointed with the medical treatment received by his client. She became suddenly and seriously ill and her resulting behaviour bore no resemblance to her usual behaviour. She went into hospital and it became clear to her social worker that nothing was going to be done for her. Hospital staff incorrectly attributed her behaviour to her mental handicap, and had the social worker not insisted that his client receive treatment she would have died. Consequently he noted, 'Health is not client's problem in handling, but convincing medics that it is worthwhile handling.' In terms of having a high medical profile, only one person in the study displays behaviour that may be described as hypochondriacal. He is well known in his locality and his social worker is accustomed to collecting him from hospitals which this man fails to persuade to admit him.

In respect of housing, 41 people have some degree of contact with housing agencies (predominantly, those living in council housing). For one group of three women, who rent their home from the social services department, their weekly visit to pay their rent is a social and enjoyable occasion. In contrast to their experience, those living in council housing who have regular contact with their housing department, do so largely to report repairs outstanding and/or to request transfer to another area. Of the handful of people who referred to their contact with the housing departments, the comments are consistently negative:

'I'm having trouble with the housing department at the moment. They don't seem to be helping me. I stutter sometimes, it's like a kid's talk. They think I'm a kid instead of a woman you see. I have an awful job with the housing [department]. I go every week. They just shut me away and said they couldn't help me. They got to help someone else you see. . . . The housing [department] people won't do it you see [that is, transfer this woman and her partner]. But these housing [department] people won't do it you see. They don't seem to get the point of it you know.'

Three people are dissatisfied that they are living in tenancies where most of their neighbours are elderly. One woman described her experiences with their housing department, who insisted that she and her husband decorate their flat before they could be considered for transfer:

'We've sent forms in and forms in and nothing's happened. . . . We decorated it twice since we've been here. We decorated it once and they said it wasn't good enough so we had to do it again. A fella come and he said "You haven't done it to our satisfaction." See he takes epileptic fits and I'm scared of him doing things like that.'

Most people in this study are in receipt of supplementary benefits and pensions. In total, 47 people have some degree of regular contact with the Department of Health and Social Security (information is missing for nineteen people). Only a few people referred to the contact they had with the DHSS, and of these, one is especially critical:

'The social pay rent, electric and heating.'

'Very unhelpful, wouldn't help me. [This woman had been mugged and had no money for food.] I said to her "I hope you'll never need help because I'll laugh if you do." I had no money and she told me to eat bread.'

SUMMARY

Support personnel have a pivotal role in the lives of people who are living in their own homes. Many people are helped in the areas in which they may never be fully independent, to enable them to continue living in their own homes. In general, the help that people receive from social services personnel corresponds to their needs. In the area of daily and leisure activities, however, the people who are retired or unemployed do not receive the same support enjoyed by their counterparts with organised daily activities. Handling finances and medical problems are the areas in which people are given most help.

Some 46 people see and/or have telephone contact with their social workers once a week or more often. Social workers are involved in many areas of their clients' lives and they are frequently regarded as friends. There is a heavy reliance on help from social services personnel. Help is negotiated and clients are treated as adults who can and do make decisions about their own lives.

The maintenance of people's independence is cited as an objective for 24 people. Social workers see increased independence as the aim for a further seventeen people. This has implications for the withdrawal of support once people achieve this. It is incompatible with the friendship role perceived by most people.

In total, 61 people are described as successful by their social workers.

The contact that a small number of people have with non-specialist agencies indicates that insensitive treatment can occur.

Part 3

Signposts

8
Signposts

Researchers who have investigated the lives of adults with mental handicap who are living independently typically conclude that people achieve satisfactory adjustments to life in the community (Cobb, 1972). This presumes that we have a clear picture of what successful community adjustment is, and that we know what features of people's lives we should examine to know whether this has been achieved. In reality, the picture is unclear. As Edgerton and Bercovici (1976) noted, '. . . we do not possess shared criteria of normal community adjustment nor do we know what persons who are labelled mentally retarded would put forward as their criteria of "normal community adjustment"' (p. 490).

It seemed that in order to unravel the complexity of community adjustment, I had to be mindful of previous research; to consider the circumstances of people living in their own homes, their observations and their concerns; and to consider the tasks and concerns of support personnel. The outcome of this process was the identification of a number of different facets of community adjustment. In combination, these facets contribute something to our understanding of the concept.

This chapter presents the findings of the further analysis of the information presented in Chapters 4 to 7. For each of the facets of community adjustment identified, the analysis has a twofold purpose: to help us to understand which people appear to be doing well, which people appear to be having difficulties and why; and to indicate signposts for further development if an intolerable burden is not to be placed on people with mental handicap, their families and service providers.

For the purposes of this chapter, the results of a series of stepwise multiple regression analyses will be presented in the following sections, each one examining specific issues. This method of analysis makes it possible to list those factors that are most closely associated with particular outcomes, such as people being satisfied with their homes, being described as successful, being in debt and being victimised. Tables detailing the analyses appear in Appendix 2. While most of these tables present powerful statistical findings, all but two will be discussed in this chapter. (Tables H and I are omitted from consideration as their predictors are poor in comparison to others.) The sequence in which the sections are presented generally corresponds to the ordering of topics in the preceding chapters.

FACTORS ASSOCIATED WITH EXPRESSIONS OF CONCERN

'I've had it up to here [tapping forehead]. I preferred it when he was in the hostel. He drinks his money and he's round at our place for meals. I've had him all me life.' (A sibling)

In Chapter 4 the concerns of social workers, relating largely to people's skills, were outlined. In the analysis, the index of concern (Table A, Appendix 2) refers to concerns reported in people's case records and it derives from three sources, social services personnel, education/training services, and families.

The analysis shows that concern is more likely to be expressed when personal cleanliness is wanting, when general deterioration is evident, and when there is evidence of excessive smoking and/or drinking. Services and families are alarmed by poor hygiene. Its consequences are immediately apparent and unpleasant. For some people it is indicative of a breakdown of household routines and/or depression. For families, it appears to be indicative of inadequate support, and is perhaps an implied criticism that independence is not appropriate for their handicapped member. Similarly, evidence of poor eating habits evokes concern. Once again the consequences are tangible in the form of weight loss or gain. The consequences of excessive smoking and drinking are especially alarming to families. Anxieties relate to the cost of maintaining these habits and the health implications, but mostly, they address the inadequacy of supervision.

Concern is also more likely to be expressed on behalf of men. In a society where attitudes, expectations and behaviour are strongly influenced by gender, this is not surprising. Perhaps social workers are responding to the stereotype of men unequal to doing housework. It is interesting that the study did not find any significant differences between the skills of men and women. Maybe it is inevitable that services and families should reinforce the role of women coping in their own homes, that is, it is appropriate for women to manage, whereas men need help.

Services tread a difficult path in enabling people to maintain themselves in their own homes. They do not have the unlimited support of their clients' families and their efforts are not necessarily going to be seen in a favourable light. Not all families and service personnel regard independent living as desirable. It conflicts with the way in which many families have reared and continue to rear their handicapped members, protecting them from an adult status and the risks that this entails. It also conflicts with the way in which some services and their personnel operate: denying people opportunities to make decisions about many areas of their lives (McKenna, 1986).

Latib, Conroy and Hess (1984) explored the resistance of families and service personnel towards deinstitutionalisation. They concluded that, 'A formal mechanism must be devised to involve all families in the deinstitutionalization process, and this cannot be done without knowing what families think' (p. 90). Similarly, the views of service personnel must be explored, '. . . the opinions and feelings of the people whose lives have been so intimately intertwined with the lives of the clients are also important' (p. 91). Latib, Conroy and Hess (1984) recommended that for each individual a forum must be provided for a hearing of the concerns of significant people prior to and throughout the community placement process. The findings presented here support their recommendations. They constitute sound initial signposts for the future.

People who are living independently require a responsive service, and their families need reassurance that their handicapped members will not be neglected. People's diets, medical condition and lifestyles change for a variety of reasons. The monitoring that a responsive service requires should be abreast of changes that do occur and should act accordingly.

FACTORS ASSOCIATED WITH FINANCIAL DIFFICULTIES

People's skills in relation to money are limited. In this section, financial difficulties are explored in two ways. Firstly, those factors associated with debts and the absence of food in the house are discussed. Secondly, the factors associated with people's satisfaction with their money and its management are explored.

Debts

> *'I'd prefer to have me own money and everything. They've taken things away from us you know. The telly, bill, gas fires. I don't seem to get on with anybody you know. It's 'cause I can't talk properly you know. . . . I've been to the DHS and tell them I've got no money. They don't seem to care.'*

The analysis shows that debts are significantly more likely to occur when people are victimised (Table B). Some seventeen people in total have had money taken from them and/or property stolen. In respect of money, this clearly impacts upon people's ability to pay bills and ensure that they have sufficient food. We must recall, however, the man who did not report having money taken from him as he was '*a bit scared*'.

Routines are an important feature of household tasks and they seem to be protective against debts. For people who do not have routines, debts are more likely to occur and these people are less likely to have money for food. It is reasonable to expect that people who do not regularly put aside a proportion of their incomes for bills are unlikely to be able to pay these.

Debts are more likely to result for people at the younger end of the age range. Arguably these people are the most inexperienced in handling money and the most likely to err in the payment of bills and the purchase of food. People are also more likely to have debts if they have no formal structure to their days, that is, if they are unemployed or retired. Given that younger people are more likely to have debts, it would seem that it is more likely to be the people who are unemployed rather than retired who are in financial straits. Finally, people who are in receipt of benefits are also more likely to find themselves in debt than people who have wages. It is intuitively reasonable that people who have more money are in a better position to pay their bills and make necessary purchases.

Social workers are attuned to money management and for most people this is supervised. To avoid financial difficulties, signposts are clear: reported incidents of hostile behaviours should not be dismissed as unfortunate. Victimisation, debts and the absence of food appear to be companions. Routines for household tasks have protective qualities and these should be encouraged. Attention has to be focused on the people who do not have any formal structure to their day and the people whose incomes are especially limited. Without this, these people may be candidates for debts and inadequately stocked households.

Satisfaction with money management

> *'Simon's [home carer] a great help really in one respect definitely. I'm able now [to collect money] yes.'*

Another way of looking at finances is to consider the views of the people concerned, and to look at the sorts of things that are associated with their expressed satisfaction in this area. It will have been gathered from Chapter 5 that a number of people have pressing needs for financial help and that some people's incomes are so low as to impose serious financial poverty. In spite of this, only twelve people spoke in negative terms about their money, and of these, six people spoke of a desire for an increase in their incomes. The majority of people were noncommittal about their finances.

Primarily, having the skills to handle relationships makes for satisfaction in money management (Table C). This is intuitively correct if we recall that 62 people share accommodation. In order to manage their finances, minimally, they have to get on together so that they can make decisions about spending. Similarly, they have to get on with their social workers who, by their own admission, are largely preoccupied with sorting out people's finances. It is also important to note that people who live in groups, generally have more money at their disposal. They can pool resources.

The analysis also shows that the people who are content with what they do during the day are also likely to express satisfaction with the management of their money. This parallels the findings reported in the first part of this section. People are more likely to have debts if they have unstructured days. We know that those who are unemployed and without any formal structure to their days are largely dissatisfied with their lot.

This section highlights an important signpost that is related to many of the topics explored in this chapter: getting on with people has many positive spinoffs and it is more likely to occur if people's views about who they want to live with are respected. In the move to close hospitals, people are largely returned to their areas of origin and sometimes this has been at cost to friendships. If friendships are not respected then there is a high probability that subsequent placements will break down (Heller, 1984). It is wrong to assume that people with compatible skills can be placed together and that a happily functioning household will result. If they are friends, and decisions about who they want to share a home with are respected, then there is more likelihood that they will be more successful in maintaining themselves and their household. We offer no favours to people in assuming that we know best.

FACTORS ASSOCIATED WITH THE CLEANLINESS OF PEOPLE'S HOMES

'Liz cleans on Friday, polishing and that and Dorothy does the dusting. I scrubbed the carpet today with some stuff and I scrubbed the two carpets upstairs on Tuesday.'

A small number of people experience difficulty in keeping their homes clean. The analysis shows that the cleanliness of people's homes is associated with the extent of household facilities, that is, having a vacuum cleaner and washing machine for example (Table D). So, as might be expected, having the means to keep your home clean is a good indicator that it will be clean. This lends support to the signpost that people's possessions are important. If they are not able to purchase items when they move into their homes, their limited incomes almost guarantee that they will be unable to buy these at a later date.

Another factor that is associated with the cleanliness of the home is contact with social workers. A small number of people resist association with their social workers in the patches when things are not going too well. This avoidance results in limited contact and a reduction in the general monitoring activity of the social worker. It is therefore reasonable to appreciate why the avoidance of social workers is associated with deterioration in the cleanliness of people's homes. Edgerton (1967) described how adults with mental handicap devoted themselves to denying their labels and to 'passing' as non mentally handicapped people. Contact with services gives people a high profile if they are receiving a lot of support. It could be argued that people who do not want help from social services personnel are trying to 'pass' independently of them. Service personnel should be aware of people's concern with this.

Brown and Hughson (1980) describe a preparation programme for independent living which makes a contract with the people concerned that they will continue to use the services that are available to them to support them. Although such a contract might only ever be referred to on behalf of a small number of people, it is an option that services may wish to consider. It cannot be an end in itself, however. The reasons for people avoiding assistance must be explored and understood if a contract is to have any meaning.

The signposts are that if people are to have clean homes, they need the means to achieve this. The general monitoring activities of support personnel ensure that the cleanliness of people's homes is likely to be maintained.

FACTORS ASSOCIATED WITH HEALTH AND HYGIENE PROBLEMS

'They were saying that drink puts weight on you, and then tablets. Well, if we do have a drink we can have a lager, in moderation . . . Me sister is diet mania. She said, "Oh you have put weight on." I said, "For God's sake shut up will you?" The nurses keep weighing us . . . we do our best for them . . . I've got anaemia. I call it the cousin to leukaemia.'

Health and hygiene problems refer to evidence of poor diet, depression, general deterioration, neglect of personal hygiene, drinking and smoking to excess and concern being expressed by medical services. The analysis shows that four factors are associated with this (Table E). Importantly, people look after themselves less well if they live in poor quality neighbourhoods. Byrne *et al.* (1986) in their investigation of health and housing in the general population, acknowledge that it is difficult to disentangle all the factors that affect people's health. In their study of 480 households they found that people living in 'difficult to let' housing areas reported more illness and inferior health status than did those people living in other housing areas; that people who live in houses are in better health than people who live in flats; and that people who live in high-rise flats were not as healthy as those living in low to medium-rise flats. This puts the association between people's health and hygiene problems and their environment in context.

Health and hygiene problems are also associated with conspicuousness. This is possibly because people who are putting on weight, neglecting their hygiene and/or not changing their clothes sufficiently often, are likely to be more conspicuous than others. It will be seen that people who are conspicuous and who live in poor neighbourhoods are more likely to be victimised. Victimisation may in turn lead to greater conspicuousness as those who experience it become depressed and fearful.

People look after themselves less well if their homes are in a poor state of repair. A small number of people live in homes that are damp; in poor repair; and at periods during their tenancies, they have had no power or water. It is not difficult to appreciate that these factors do impinge upon people's health and hygiene and have an overall depressing effect.

Finally, people look after themselves less well if they are dissatisfied with their daily activities. It is reasonable to assume that dissatisfaction with most of our waking hours is associated with depression and the tendency to be less aware of health and hygiene. Unemployment and retirement do not yield valued status. Given some people's preferences for ordinary jobs, it is not surprising that those who are disappointed in this area of their lives may neglect themselves to their detriment.

People who are unemployed have poorer health and there are costs to them and to health and social services. People who do not have the social contact, enhanced self-image and financial advantage of work (Florian, 1982), and whose days are not structured, are more at risk for debts and dissatisfaction with leisure as well as problems with health and hygiene.

The signposts are that people should not be placed on disreputable estates in poor quality housing. We have to be attuned to the consequences of people's appearance and the fact that there is an association between victimisation and conspicuousness. Finally, support services should be particularly focused on people whose days lack any formal structure.

FACTORS ASSOCIATED WITH SATISFACTION WITH DAILY ACTIVITIES

'I've got me friends in work . . . Maureen and Monica are friends I work with [at a book binders]. There's a cutter for the books [on a photo] and that's Nora and Beryl, another friend of mine. That's the boss and that's the table with the books on.'

Information about people's satisfaction with their daily activities was gathered from the interviews. The analysis suggests that three factors in particular are associated with this (Table F). Primarily, having routines for household tasks is indicative of satisfaction with daily activities. It appears that the benefits of routines and the order that they impose on our lives affect satisfaction. It should be noted, however, that highly rigid routines or 'changelessness' is associated with stress (Boyce *et al.*, 1977). Somewhere between the chaos which results from a total lack of routines and the rigidity of highly enforced routines, we ought to be able to help people to organise their lives in a way that is flexible and ultimately satisfying.

The people who enjoy and seek contact with their social workers are more likely to be satisfied with their daily activities. The majority of people enjoy the company of their social workers and regard them as friends. Daily activities are seemingly regarded in a more positive light if they are either to be shared with a social worker, or if they are to be described to a social worker who is friendly, encouraging and interested.

Lastly, people who live in houses are more likely to express satisfaction with their daily activities than their counterparts who live in flats. This appears to relate to the fact that, in general, houses are in more desirable and attractive areas than flats. Given that 44 people are perhaps compelled to spend a lot of their time at home by virtue of being unemployed or retired, then immediate environments invariably contribute to people's satisfactions.

The signposts are that having household routines has positive consequences. People may need encouragement to establish and/or maintain these. The importance of regular contact with support personnel cannot be underestimated. Once again, people's location in certain types of housing and localities is not an incidental concern. It impacts on many areas of people's lives.

FACTORS ASSOCIATED WITH SATISFACTORY RELATIONSHIPS WITH PEOPLE

The area of interpersonal issues was examined in two ways. In the first part of this section, evidence of positive relationships with people is considered. In the second part of the section, people's satisfaction with their interpersonal relations is explored.

Positive relationships

'I go out shopping then I go out to friends in the afternoon. I go shopping every day and I go to friends every day – different people . . . everybody knows me 'round here. I tell you, I'm sociable. I like to be sociable.'

Information about positive relationships was derived from three sources: people's case records; information from social workers; and the interviews. The index of positive relationships includes having visitors, not experiencing loneliness and having enjoyable relationships with friends and neighbours (Table G). The analysis shows that five factors are associated with having positive relationships. Of these, the absence of victimisation is important. Once again, evidence regarding the extent to which victimisation impinges negatively upon people's lives is highlighted. Arguably, people who experience victimisation are unable to trust others and, regarding themselves as prey, they do not or cannot take the necessary steps to form relationships. Some people are too frightened to leave their homes, and inevitably this reduces their opportunities to meet others.

It is interesting that positive relationships are associated with not having lived in a tenancy for an extended period. In the early days of moving into their own homes, people receive a lot of help and have many visits from support personnel. They are encouraged to participate in local activities. The visits of social workers reduce as confidence and competence increases. Without the support of their social worker, and once the initial enthusiasm of living independently has been tempered by lack of money, lack of occupation and/or poor housing, people may reduce their efforts to meet others.

Women have more positive relationships than men. However, the women in this sample are no more skilled than men in terms of their rated ability in interpersonal relationships. One way of understanding this difference is to consider the different socialisation patterns and practices of men and women. A role assumed by women is that of caring for others (Belle, 1982). Women develop to accommodate the needs of others, often at their own expense. Under stress, women may seek comfort and advice from others because they have a personal sense of how much help can come from others, and also because they can develop 'affectively richer' relationships than men (Aries and Johnson, 1983; Olson and McCubbin, 1983; Burda, Vaux and Schill, 1984). In contrast, men tend to keep problems to themselves (Rutter, 1981; Stokes and Wilson, 1984). A further possible explanation for the association between positive relations and women concerns the reactions of non-handicapped people towards people with mental handicap. Possibly, women are seen as less threatening and frightening than men and this may influence and temper people's approaches to them.

People who are limited in terms of their abilities in being with and dealing with others are less likely to enjoy positive personal relationships. Interpersonal/social skill deficits are regarded as obstacles to people embarking on training for independent living. Foss, Bostwick and Harris (1978) found that the people with mental handicap they interviewed expressed a high degree of concern regarding their interpersonal/social skills deficits. This information was used to target services more effectively to these people's needs. Not everybody is limited in this sphere, however; 40 people are reckoned by their social workers to be able to handle interpersonal relationships. For the remainder, dissatisfaction with interpersonal relationships seems possible.

Lastly, people who do not avoid their social workers are in a more favourable position than those who do. It seems likely that social workers' concerns for their clients' social lives means that they guide their clients to agencies and facilities where they might meet others, they liaise with families and they are regarded as friends themselves. These opportunities are unavailable to people who avoid their social workers.

Satisfaction with interpersonal relations

'We always got on, didn't we? Now and again we might fall out, but it's not often. . . . Me sister-in-law said, "You don't find things going smooth all the time, even in normal households." Mrs Cassidy, she put the two best ones together. [Formerly lived with Jackie.] She's really mentally handicapped is Jackie. She wouldn't do anything for us in the house. Nothing. It took her all her time to make a cup of tea. Wouldn't do anything for us yet we used to do anything for her.'

Another way of looking at interpersonal issues focuses on what people say about their relationships and how satisfied they appear to be with these. Satisfaction refers to people's views about their neighbours, the people who visit them and their living situation, that is, whether they live alone or with others (Table J). The analysis demonstrates that three factors are associated with people's satisfaction. Firstly, people who are victimised are unlikely to express satisfaction with their interpersonal relations. As indicated in Part 1 and other sections, the influence of victimisation is consistently damaging.

Further, as in Part 1, being unskilled in interpersonal issues is associated with dissatisfaction with interpersonal relationships. Finally, people whose days are not structured are more likely to express dissatisfaction with their interpersonal relationships than those who have the structure of either employment (open or sheltered), the ATC, college or voluntary work. Once again, it appears that unemployment and retirement do not reap many advantages for people.

The signposts from this section are that evidence of victimisation should always be acted upon. When support personnel 'fade out' they are missed by their clients. Services must question the appropriateness of ceasing to visit people on a regular basis. Training and guidance in interpersonal skills should precede and continue throughout people's placements. The way in which people spend their days affects the quality of many aspects of their lives. People who are occupied during the day fare better than those who are not.

FACTORS ASSOCIATED WITH SATISFACTION WITH THE HOME AND LOCATION

'I don't mind the flat, it's just the area that I can't settle in. . . . I'd like to move off and get back to where I come from.'

Looking at people's satisfaction with where they live, we need to remember that 22 people live in tenancies that may be described as 'hard to let' and the living circumstances of fourteen of these people are especially dire. When people talked about their homes and neighbourhoods, 31 expressed dissatisfaction, and of these seventeen said that they wanted to move. In contrast, 38 people expressed satisfaction with their homes.

The analysis demonstrates that the absence of victimisation is the main indicator of satisfaction (Table K). Previous sections have indicated the pervasive effects of victimisation. We know that it affects the way in which people see themselves and others. It also impinges on their views of their homes and locality. For people who experience victimisation, they are fearful for their own safety in their neighbourhoods and their homes become their prisons.

Of the four other factors that are associated with satisfaction with the home and location, the extent of people's household facilities is important; that is, the more facilities that people have, the more likely they are to express satisfaction. Table 5.4 (Chapter 5) fleshes out this picture. Extensive household facilities refer to the possession of all or most of the items on this table.

Satisfaction is more likely to result if people's homes are in a decent state of repair. In Chapter 5 it is reported that the homes of the majority of people are in a good state of repair. For the people whose homes have rising damp, loose brickwork and/or badly fitting windows, in other words, features that are indicative of physical deterioration, dissatisfaction is likely to result.

The number of moves people have had since living independently also affects satisfaction. While most people have been fairly static, seven people have had three or more changes of tenancies. It is this type of instability that is indicative of dissatisfaction with home and location. The signpost is that services should monitor people's satisfaction with their homes and neighbourhoods. While the analysis does not imply that people should remain in their initial tenancies at all costs, it highlights the importance of attending to the reputation of particular areas and the state of repair of prospective tenancies. It is the experience of people in this study that repair work does not appear to be a priority of housing departments.

Finally, it is interesting to note that the 26 people who live alone are more likely to express satisfaction with their homes than those who live with others. Perhaps it is the case that privacy, unknown in the lives of many people with mental handicap, is valued and a source of particular satisfaction. Perhaps also, people who live in hospitals and hostels cannot build up personal possessions in the same way as those with their own homes. Having your own home entails having belongings that do not have to be shared. Conceivably these advantages contribute to single people's satisfaction with their own homes.

The attitude of people to their localities is the subject of increasing literature in sociology and community psychology (scc, for example, Ladewig and McCann, 1980). A recent model of community satisfaction relates people's perceptions of their local community to their places within social networks (see, for example, Heller et al., 1981; Bardo, 1984). Victimisation lowers the quality of people's lives and imposes restrictions on them. The precautions that some people take restrict their lives and reduce their opportunities for meeting others. This supports the model of community satisfaction described above.

People leaving hospitals and hostels do not need removal vans to transfer their belongings. By the time most of us have attained adulthood we have accumulated belongings. We may have bought or inherited possessions or received these as gifts. It seems that possessions for most people in this study are a recent phenomenon and their appreciation of these is reflected in this section. Recalling the man whose dissatisfaction with the hostel in which he lived hinged upon his inability to keep his stereo system safe, an inevitable signpost results: having possessions in your own home is valued.

FACTORS ASSOCIATED WITH VICTIMISATION

'Kids – I wouldn't let them in now. I've been told so many times by the police to avoid them. I had a fiver in me purse one night – it got nicked. . . . Social worker tells me to be careful all the time, who I let in. You never know, do you?. . . . I've had letters through me door threatening to kill me cat. It's frightened me.'

Victimisation in this study embraces physical and verbal abuse, intimidation from neighbours, damage to home and property, having property stolen and/or having money taken. Throughout this chapter it is clear that victimisation impinges on many areas of people's lives and on many facets of community adjustment. The consequences are invariably negative.

Three factors are particularly associated with victimisation (Table L). The most significant of these is a person's environment. The people who live in poor quality neighbourhoods (near disused houses, where rubbish is uncollected, where buildings are daubed with graffiti, remote from services and facilities, and in flats/houses with depressed rateable values), are more likely to experience victimisation. This finding corroborates Purkis and Hodson's (1982) contention: '. . . when complexes built to high standards lie vandalised, demoralised and boarded up [they are] no place for anyone, let alone those with disabilities and other difficulties' (p. 33). Good housing in desirable areas is not universally enjoyed by everybody. Accepting houses in 'hard to let' tenancies on behalf of people with mental handicap, or allowing clients to accept tenancies in these localities, should not occur. Services should know which areas are rated as poor and which are the unpopular estates and tenancies. Ideally, people should see areas and tenancies at different times of the day and note whether a prospective tenancy is near a corner by which youngsters gather, for example. Attention should also be paid to the proximity of local schools. School children do not have a creditable history of association with the people I met, and services should be conscious of many people's fear of children and youngsters.

Williams, Sewel and Twine (1986) have shown that people with low incomes are channelled into housing areas which are perceived as being the least desirable. This stark finding is of particular pertinence to people with mental handicap, who are poorly represented in the workforce and have low incomes. Knowing that there is a strong association between victimisation and living in poor quality areas reiterates an earlier signpost: there are powerful reasons for ensuring that people are not allocated tenancies in poor areas.

People's appearance also plays a part in the likelihood of their being victimised. The people who are conspicuous are more likely to experience victimisation, either on a one-off or a repeat basis. Appearance is an important factor in the acceptance of people with mental handicap in community settings (Wolfensberger, 1972; Sherrill, 1980). There is evidence to suggest that people with mental handicap who are overweight are likely to be the objects of increased social prejudice and non-acceptance (Rotatori, Switzky and Fox, 1983). Studies suggest that excessive body weight and posture problems are prevalent conditions among adults with mental handicap in general (Sherrill, 1980; Emery *et al.*, 1985) and it seems that being overweight is a particular problem for women with mental handicap (Fox and Rotatori, 1982). Given the serious health implications of being overweight, services should be alert to this problem: providing support to people who are trying to lose weight; ensuring that training in nutrition is provided; and helping people to understand the consequences of eating and activity patterns, for example.

Sherrill (1980) reports that a number of strategies are effective in ameliorating posture patterns in children with mental handicap: peer modelling; behaviour management techniques; body awareness activities; relaxation training; and sociodrama. Given that some people are conspicuous by their posture and the way in which they walk, this study provides compelling evidence to indicate that training in self-presentation should be an integral part of preparation for community living.

Finally, people who are at the younger end of the age range are more likely to experience victimisation. Perhaps this is indicative of younger people's unfamiliarity with their current lifestyles and locations, and their lack of 'street wisdom'. Perhaps also there is a greater tolerance of what may be seen as different, eccentric or conspicuous behaviour in older people and therefore less likelihood of unscrupulous individuals regarding them as fair game. There is evidence to suggest that criminal victimisation is relatively low in the older population. It is believed that the lifestyles of older people present fewer opportunities for victimisation (Cook *et al.*, 1978; Liang and Sengstock, 1981).

The signposts are that people should not be expected to remain in houses/flats and neighbourhoods where they are being victimised. Training in assertion and self-presentation should be an integral part of preparation for community living.

FACTORS ASSOCIATED WITH SOCIAL WORKERS' RATINGS OF SUCCESS

'All we want is someone to help us put the [light] bulbs in because we can do anything, us two, practically. . . . It's heaven here.

The final facet of community adjustment explored was social workers' ratings of success (Table M). They described 61 people as 'successful'. As social workers had no guidance as to how they were to make this rating, inevitably they used different criteria. For example, one social worker rated all his clients as successful. He explained that as these people had spent many years in institutions, the fact that they were managing in their own homes demonstrated their success. Other social workers used criteria based on such factors as increased independence of services and involvement in community activities. Social workers' ratings of success are not the most important facet of community adjustment examined in the study. They must be seen in combination with all the other facets described.

It appears that people are more likely to be described as successful by their social workers if they are without debts. Debts jeopardise the stability of people's lives.

The people who expressed satisfaction with their housework are the ones more likely to be described as successful by their social workers. And people are more likely to be described as successful if they live in good quality neighbourhoods. This confirms earlier findings that living in poor quality areas is detrimental to people's lives.

Lastly, people who are content with the management of their money are more likely to be regarded as successful. It is important to recall that skills in handling relationships and satisfaction with daily activities are both associated with satisfaction with the management of money.

Confirming the earlier observation that success has a multifaceted nature, in this study we have seen that a number of factors are associated with the rating of success: not being in debt; not being victimised; having structured days and routines for household tasks; having a wage; being satisfied with household tasks; having had few changes of tenancy; being skilled in interpersonal relations; living in a good-quality neighbourhood; and being satisfied with money management and daily activities. Overall, the people who were described as less than successful were also those experiencing difficulties in the areas already examined in this chapter. This points to the fact that social workers are attuned to the salient difficulties.

SUMMARY AND IMPLICATIONS

This chapter draws conclusions from the study to suggest signposts for planners and support service personnel. It appears that there are six areas that merit particular attention: (1) preparation for independent living; (2) skills in handling relationships; (3) structured days and routines for household tasks; (4) victimisation; (5) a cluster of disadvantages consisting of poor quality tenancies, debts and inadequate resources; and (6) support.

Preparation for independent living

(1) People must be involved in discussions about who they are going to live with. Their friendships and preferences must be respected.

(2) A forum must be provided for exploring the concerns of significant people prior to and throughout the placement process. This must include the people who are to be placed as well as their families. Families are potentially a significant support system and their views matter if the person with a mental handicap wishes them to be sought.

It appears that people are more likely to be described as successful by their social workers if they are without debts. Debts jeopardise the stability of people's lives.

The people who expressed satisfaction with their housework are the ones more likely to be described as successful by their social workers. And people are more likely to be described as successful if they live in good quality neighbourhoods. This confirms earlier findings that living in poor quality areas is detrimental to people's lives.

Lastly, people who are content with the management of their money are more likely to be regarded as successful. It is important to recall that skills in handling relationships and satisfaction with daily activities are both associated with satisfaction with the management of money.

Confirming the earlier observation that success has a multifaceted nature, in this study we have seen that a number of factors are associated with the rating of success: not being in debt; not being victimised; having structured days and routines for household tasks; having a wage; being satisfied with household tasks; having had few changes of tenancy; being skilled in interpersonal relations; living in a good-quality neighbourhood; and being satisfied with money management and daily activities. Overall, the people who were described as less than successful were also those experiencing difficulties in the areas already examined in this chapter. This points to the fact that social workers are attuned to the salient difficulties.

SUMMARY AND IMPLICATIONS

This chapter draws conclusions from the study to suggest signposts for planners and support service personnel. It appears that there are six areas that merit particular attention: (1) preparation for independent living; (2) skills in handling relationships; (3) structured days and routines for household tasks; (4) victimisation; (5) a cluster of disadvantages consisting of poor quality tenancies, debts and inadequate resources; and (6) support.

Preparation for independent living

(1) People must be involved in discussions about who they are going to live with. Their friendships and preferences must be respected.

(2) A forum must be provided for exploring the concerns of significant people prior to and throughout the placement process. This must include the people who are to be placed as well as their families. Families are potentially a significant support system and their views matter if the person with a mental handicap wishes them to be sought.

facilities that people have, the more likely they are to express satisfaction. Table 5.4 (Chapter 5) fleshes out this picture. Extensive household facilities refer to the possession of all or most of the items on this table.

Satisfaction is more likely to result if people's homes are in a decent state of repair. In Chapter 5 it is reported that the homes of the majority of people are in a good state of repair. For the people whose homes have rising damp, loose brickwork and/or badly fitting windows, in other words, features that are indicative of physical deterioration, dissatisfaction is likely to result.

The number of moves people have had since living independently also affects satisfaction. While most people have been fairly static, seven people have had three or more changes of tenancies. It is this type of instability that is indicative of dissatisfaction with home and location. The signpost is that services should monitor people's satisfaction with their homes and neighbourhoods. While the analysis does not imply that people should remain in their initial tenancies at all costs, it highlights the importance of attending to the reputation of particular areas and the state of repair of prospective tenancies. It is the experience of people in this study that repair work does not appear to be a priority of housing departments.

Finally, it is interesting to note that the 26 people who live alone are more likely to express satisfaction with their homes than those who live with others. Perhaps it is the case that privacy, unknown in the lives of many people with mental handicap, is valued and a source of particular satisfaction. Perhaps also, people who live in hospitals and hostels cannot build up personal possessions in the same way as those with their own homes. Having your own home entails having belongings that do not have to be shared. Conceivably these advantages contribute to single people's satisfaction with their own homes.

The attitude of people to their localities is the subject of increasing literature in sociology and community psychology (see, for example, Ladewig and McCann, 1980). A recent model of community satisfaction relates people's perceptions of their local community to their places within social networks (see, for example, Heller et al., 1981; Bardo, 1984). Victimisation lowers the quality of people's lives and imposes restrictions on them. The precautions that some people take restrict their lives and reduce their opportunities for meeting others. This supports the model of community satisfaction described above.

People leaving hospitals and hostels do not need removal vans to transfer their belongings. By the time most of us have attained adulthood we have accumulated belongings. We may have bought or inherited possessions or received these as gifts. It seems that possessions for most people in this study are a recent phenomenon and their appreciation of these is reflected in this section. Recalling the man whose dissatisfaction with the hostel in which he lived hinged upon his inability to keep his stereo system safe, an inevitable signpost results: having possessions in your own home is valued.

(3) Families need regular reassurance and evidence that their handicapped members are not neglected at any time.

(4) Training in assertion and self-presentation should be an integral part of preparation for independent living. Guidance in these areas should continue throughout people's placements (see, for example, Bregman, 1985).

(5) Training and guidance in interpersonal skills should precede and continue throughout people's placements. One way of accomplishing this is by using a role model/mentor, perhaps a citizen advocate or volunteer befriender. The befriender could help a person to develop a range of appropriate responses to different social situations and give guidance on social norms and social niceties, for example (Atkinson and Ward, 1986).

(6) People should be aware of some of the varying difficulties they may encounter, for example, managing money; dealing with name calling; dealing with official correspondence. They need reassurance and evidence that it is all right for them to seek help.

(7) People need to know who to contact when they need help, especially outside office hours. Telephones are essential if people are not to live in fear on estates of 'hard to let' tenancies.

(8) People should be encouraged to have routines for their household tasks and money management.

(9) Hospitals and hostels do not have reputations for paying attention to nutritious diets and body maintenance. Training in basic health education is important. People trying to lose weight, for example, need some understanding of nutrition, dietary restrictions and exercise.

Skills in handling relationships

(1) People with mental handicap leaving hospitals and hostels do not have the opportunities to develop a range of social contacts and relationships and they mostly regard their social workers as their friends. Support personnel should devote time to exploring ways of integrating people in the lives of their localities.

(2) Some hostels provide aftercare and support and others do not. Aftercare is reasonable given that many people have spent long periods of their lives in staffed accommodation. People should be encouraged to maintain contact with friends and staff from hospitals or hostels. Some people will need help to do so.

(3) People need practice in order to be skilled in handling relationships and they cannot get this if they have nothing to do and/or nowhere to go.

(4) People who are frightened in their homes and neighbourhoods as a result of victimisation have no opportunities to develop interpersonal skills.

(5) The appointment of foster/befriender neighbours may make the transition to independent living easier for some people.

(6) The appointment of foster/befriender families/couples/individuals with whom people can stay occasionally may relieve some of the pressures on support personnel.

Structured days and routines for household tasks

(1) People who have structured days and routines for their household tasks fare rather better than those who do not.

(2) People opt out of adult training centres and work experience for which they are inadequately paid (and sometimes poorly treated). People mostly want a 'real' job. Pursuit of leisure is restricted because of poverty.

(3) ATCs should reconsider their roles in respect of the growing population of people living independently. Staff could be teaching essential skills such as money management; people could be working as peer tutors; the ATC could act as a bridge for ordinary neighbourhood facilities, open and sheltered employment, leisure facilities, clubs, colleges, churches, voluntary organisations, conservation projects, MSC courses, and adult education classes.

(4) Some people do not want to attend ATCs and the options listed above should be made available to them in other ways, perhaps using support personnel, volunteer befrienders, citizen advocates and peripatetic instructors. The major advantage of peripatetic instructors is that they can offer realistic teaching in people's homes.

(5) People who want a job should be in contact with disablement resettlement officers (DROs), specialist employment officers (SEOs) or pathway officers (POs). Services need to access comprehensive special employment services for disabled people.

(6) People must be encouraged to establish and maintain routines for their household tasks and money management. Routines have protective qualities.

Victimisation

(1) The consequences of victimisation are wholly negative and wide-reaching. In order to reduce the possibility of this happening, services need to know which areas are rated as poor and which are the unpopular estates.

(2) People must not be placed in 'hard to let' tenancies in disreputable areas.

(3) Reported incidents of victimisation should not be dismissed as unfortunate. The option of transferring people to different tenancies must be employed and guidance in dealing with varieties of victimisation provided. It is important that people are not unnecessarily conspicuous.

(4) Attention must be paid to people's appearance and the condition of people's clothes. People need good quality clothing. Also, they need to be capable of, or assisted in, attending to personal hygiene before they can make real choices about the way they present themselves.

(5) Tenancies close to schools should be avoided.

(6) Prospective tenancies should be seen at different times of the day to see whether they are close to meeting points for local children and youngsters.

(7) Greater use should be made of housing association property. The people I

met in housing association property were always well catered for and resided in good quality areas.

(8) Support personnel need to be aware of the possibility that victimisation may be unreported as it is distressing and discrediting. They should be alert to such cues as changes in people's lifestyles and appearance, despondency, avoidance and no money.

(9) Support personnel need to monitor what people say about their homes and neighbourhoods on a regular basis.

A cluster of disadvantages

(1) Financial support available to people moving into their own homes from hostels is inadequate (£75 to furnish a tenancy at the time of writing). It is unjust to expect people to furnish and maintain their homes on basic benefits when we reflect on the way new 'Care in the Community' schemes are financed. Financial poverty is a reality for people who are in receipt of benefits and it has far-reaching consequences. People who are in receipt of benefits are candidates for debts and inadequately stocked households.

(2) People mostly need help with money management and this is especially the case if they are in receipt of benefits. Support personnel need to be familiar with people's financial circumstances, consult with welfare rights officers and guide accordingly.

(3) Services should ensure that prospective tenancies are in a good state of repair and that they are maintained.

(4) Tenancies should be insured and well-stocked in terms of household equipment and these should be new with guarantees and service contracts. Few people in receipt of benefits will be able to buy household equipment at a later date.

(5) Residential services should consider the possibility of people bringing belongings other than clothes with them. People value their possessions and yet have limited resources to make purchases for their homes.

Support

(1) Support should not cease as a result of people's increased competence. A responsive service must be ongoing.

(2) Contact with support personnel is valued and social workers are often regarded as friends. The withdrawal of support is inappropriate and incompatible with the way in which people see their social workers. It is essential that the role of volunteer befrienders and citizen advocates, accountable to support personnel, is explored in relation to people living independently.

(3) People were very critical of their experiences in residential care. Mostly they did not wish to return. This partly explains why they tended not to complain

excessively or even sufficiently when asked about their current living circumstances. Services must be aware of this and remain attuned to people's circumstances to ensure that these do not deteriorate.

(4) Support should be particularly focused on people who are unemployed or retired. The lack of structure to their days renders them vulnerable to debts, dissatisfaction with relationships, and dissatisfaction with both money management and leisure activities.

(5) People value the privacy that independent living promotes. This should always be respected.

(6) People value being treated as adults who can and do make decisions about their own lives. This should always be expected of support personnel working with people living independently.

(7) People value the negotiation of assistance with the management of their lifestyles and homes. Negotiation should be the hallmark of support services.

(8) Services must be responsive and sensitive in their dealings with the few people who want contact with formal support personnel to discontinue and alternative, non-specialist services alerted – home helps, for example.

(9) Women are vulnerable to sex role stereotypes. Services should be attuned to the possibility that women may not receive the service that men receive.

(10) It is important to explore ways of gathering the views of people with mental handicap. Service personnel must be familiar with methods that are available and must be aware of how to seek clarification when messages are unclear.

9

The Future

'I went to France and we travelled on and we did it in one day and came back. . . . It's nice to think you can just put a pound away. . . . I liked Paris. . . . I think no matter where you go, you're always glad to get home aren't you? No place like home.'

This book has drawn together the experiences of 88 people who are living independently. It records their formidable achievements and suggests signposts to policy-makers and services if we are to learn from their experiences. The findings describe a heterogeneous, active and mostly capable population, many of whom require assistance to varying degrees to enable them to remain in their own homes.

Most people with mental handicap are not brought up to believe that they will take their place in adult society. Many people are infantilised, experiencing extended parenting long after this has ceased to be appropriate (Card, 1983; Flynn and Saleem, 1986; Richardson and Ritchie, 1986). Opportunities for association with non mentally handicapped people are reduced as a result of the sheltered settings in which their education and training takes place. The consequences of such exclusion and infantalisation, coupled with a poor self-image, are economic, physical and social dependency or powerlessness.

Independent living drastically changes this view of people with mental handicap and it raises new expectations for them. Independent living is about living in a way that is consistent with one's own preferences and values. Nearly everybody I met was adamant that they did not wish to reside in any form of staffed accommodation. Hospitals, hostels and staffed group homes cannot ignore this sobering message.

The government is busily promoting the innovation and growth of community based services for people with mental handicap. As Towell (1988) has argued, this growth spurt should not ignore: the full representation of clients' views; the importance of participation in activities with non mentally handicapped people; and the need to 'build-in' a capacity for dynamic evolution in innovative service provision. The development of large-scale services (as opposed to pioneer, well-resourced and small-scale ventures) requires a national policy and the support of the higher tiers of government.

This study brings together the unique perspectives of people with mental handicap and their social workers. Relationships are the core of the quality of life and it is clear that support personnel play a central role in their clients' lives. Social workers/community nurses/family aides/home carers and home helps are the first port of call for most people living independently and their powers and responsibilities are phenomenal. We have seen that support personnel are engaged in a multiplicity of tasks and that clients rely on them to protect their interests, assist them with household tasks and, not least of all, to be mentors and friends. Not all of the tasks are of equal value but all of them are difficult for one person to fulfil. It is essential to prepare people to be as independent as possible and it is just as vital to support people who may not be as independent as others. It appears that people's competencies may oscillate as a result of their changing circumstances. This study has indicated that a long-term safety net is a prerequisite of maintaining people in their own homes.

We have to be concerned about the inherent problems that independent living for people with mental handicap imposes on support personnel. The problems of some people are rooted in pernicious social circumstances: residence in 'hard to let' tenancies and depressed areas; financial poverty; few friends; unstructured days; and, in some types of areas, with honourable exceptions, a vicious and hostile 'community'. Against such a backcloth, can it ever be realistic to expect support personnel to end support? The study provides powerful evidence for ensuring that people are not placed in disreputable areas. Only when this becomes established practice and financial poverty ceases to be synonymous with being in receipt of benefits will we begin to feel confident that people can be adequately sustained in their own homes.

Support personnel mostly afford their clients adult status, but inevitably there is an asymmetry of power. They can control the flow of information, making it possible for one woman in the study to believe that she was unable to live with her male friend because she would lose all her benefits. They can make decisions that exclude the people most affected, for example the couple whose social worker ceased to visit as they had achieved a high level of self-sufficiency. This suggests that the concept of 'independence' is somewhat awry when the provision of assistance is monitored by the providers rather than the consumers. Arguably independence is achieved when consumers are able to negotiate and terminate assistance as necessary.

The pressures on staff to enhance the competencies of their clients and then withdraw are difficult to countenance. They are aware that their clients' social networks are wanting and that some people experience isolation and loneliness. As the signposts have indicated, support should not fade out of existence. This is especially pertinent to people who want their contact with support personnel to continue.

Support personnel appreciate the tension between facilitating people's independence and decision-making, and at the same time assisting some people in ways that are overtly directive, such as using behavioural methods to teach skills.

It is expected that they should strike a balance between assisting as advocates and encouraging people to take responsibility for their own lives. Independence is a fundamental value and it is the converse to being obliged to live your life as others want it to be lived (Turnbull and Turnbull, 1985). We know that compliance with external controllers is one of the hallmarks of the experiences of people with mental handicap (Guess, 1984; Flynn *et al.*, 1986). We know also that making our own decisions has the potential for decreasing compliance and that conflicts of interest may result. Conflicts may be most likely to occur in the areas of sexuality and its expressions and decisions about having a child and childrearing. The extension of the principle of social role valorisation to sexuality, homosexuality and childrearing is not readily accepted and yet these issues affect the lives of a significant number of the people I met. As people's uniqueness renders generalisations inappropriate, it is essential that we are openminded. These and other issues are part and parcel of living in unsupervised settings.

While it would be naive to hope that the tensions of supporting people living independently can ever be totally resolved, support personnel need opportunities to exchange experiences and insights and training, if their work is to be satisfying, if they are not to 'burn out' and they are to be active in creating the knowledge and theoretical basis for practice. Many people are deeply committed to their work, they involve their families in the lives of their clients, and consequently they are vulnerable. The support personnel I met are dedicated. They have a lot of knowledge and experience and investment in them will lead to a better service.

This study has produced little evidence that people's social and leisure activities are priorities in their preparation for independent living. Most leisure and all social activities by definition are not enjoyable alone. Is it that interpretations of normalisation have blurred our vision in our aim to ensure that people associate with non mentally handicapped people? Whatever our labels we all need a varied range of contacts and relationships with other people. Why is it that friendships in hospitals and hostels are insufficiently valued by professionals, making it possible to break up partners and groups? Some of the people I met do not enjoy association with other people with mental handicap. They are ashamed of their group membership and label and they do not feel group loyalty. We must all share the responsibility for this.

There is merit in promoting opportunities for people living independently to meet and share experiences if they wish to do so. They should be encouraged to appreciate and value each other's insights. There are many varieties of self-help groups consisting of people drawn together as a result of common experiences. It follows that opportunities to share experiences and ways of coping may have the additional merit of encouraging supportive relationships to develop. Such groups have the potential of becoming the focal point for self-advocacy, alerting us to unmet needs. Self-advocacy is a way for people to assert themselves rather than having their interests advanced by others.

While the study has shown that victimisation is more likely to occur when people are placed in depressed areas, we must not ignore the different forms of oppression that some people experience from services. Is callous treatment in hospitals and DHSS offices a necessary consequence of different intellectual endowment? Why are support personnel more concerned about men than women when the study has not found any significant differences between their skills? How can we prepare people for a world that sometimes excludes and insults? The answer would not appear to lie in the perpetuation of their segregation.

People in a culture of poverty produce little wealth, they make little use of banks and they have a low level of literacy and education. Chronic unemployment is synonymous with a low income, no savings and a shortage of money. These factors reduce the possibility of people's participation in the economic system, regardless of their intellectual capacity. People with mental handicap do not have a history of protesting. Although this study presented people with an opportunity to talk about their lives and circumstances, it appears that in the main, people do not express a great deal of dissatisfaction when this is merited. The topics of housing, neighbourhoods and daily activities evoked some strong views and biting criticisms. On the matter of housing and location, this is a matter on which there can be no compromise: people must have decent housing in areas where they are not fearful for their safety.

Open employment is rare. ATCs represent the primary service option available but questions about their direction must be addressed. Although it is over ten years since the National Development Group (1977) produced *Day Services for Mentally Handicapped Adults*, I gathered little evidence of their recommended developments during this study. People attending ATCs are mostly involved in contract work, and if their centres do operate independent living training programmes, the people I met are not participants. They were either too able for them or were graduates of them and there seemed to be no recognition that further progress was merited. There is a strong case for training people who need help with skills for independent living and arguably ATCs are one service that might accomplish this. People vote with their feet, however, and it is significant that many have opted to leave or retire from them. Why are there no peripatetic staff to teach people skills for independent living in their own homes? People do not want a respite day service, they want jobs. Why are there so few workers' cooperatives when there is transparent evidence that they benefit many workers? (Sikking, 1986). None of the people I met are on the staff of ATCs or involved in the training of people in independent living skills. There is nobody on an MSC course or who has been on one. A handful of people are known to careers officers. Disablement resettlement officers, specialist employment officers or pathway officers do not feature in people's lives. Is it because we know that in a period of recession people with mental handicap bear an even greater burden than the rest of us? This study provides tangible justification for ensuring and accessing comprehensive special employment services for disabled people. We know that a disproportionate number of them are unemployed (Gladstone, 1985).

This study suggests that independent living does not offer a status of equality with non mentally handicapped people, but it is valued nonetheless. Just over a quarter of the people I met have been objects of ridicule and violence and yet they still want to remain in their own homes. Their scope for employment, let alone occupational advancement, is limited and yet the hope of work remains for many. Overall, people's social networks are a cause for concern. These are real problems but they do not suggest that the goal of independent living for people with mental handicap should be abandoned.

We have to act on all of the issues addressed in this chapter and the preceding chapter, otherwise the outlook for these people and others who wish to live independently is bleak. Services supporting people living independently need to embed the consumer perspective within them. They need adequate staffing, opportunities to reflect on their practice and 'fine-tuning' over time in anticipation of new challenges as well as changing needs and conditions. We must listen to the people with whom we profess to be working.

References

Aanes, D. and Haagenson, L. (1978) Normalization: attention to a conceptual disaster. *Mental Retardation* **16**, 55–6.

Adams, G. R. (1977) Physical attractiveness research. *Human Development* **20**, 217–239.

Alaszewski, A. (1986) *Institutional Care and the Mentally Handicapped: The Mental Handicap Hospital*. London: Croom Helm.

Alwin, D. F., Converse, P. E. and Martin, S. S. (1985) Living arrangements and social integration. *Journal of Marriage and the Family* **May**, 319–334.

Argyle, M. (1969) *Social Interaction*. London: Tavistock Publications Ltd.

Aries, E. J. and Johnson, F. L. (1983) Close friendship in adulthood: conversational content between same-sex friends. *Sex Roles* **9**, 1183–1196.

Asher, C. C. (1984) The impact of social support networks on mental health. *Medical Care* **22**, 349–359.

Atkinson, D. (1980) Moving out of mental handicap hospitals. *APEX Journal of the British Institute of Mental Handicap* **8**, 76–78.

Atkinson, D. and Ward, L. (1986) A part of the community: social integration and neighbourhood networks. *Talking Points*, No. 3. London: Campaign for People with Mental Handicaps.

Atkinson, D. and Ward, L. (1987) Friends and Neighbours: relationships and opportunities in the community for people with a mental handicap. In N. Malin (ed.) *Reassessing Community Care: with Particular Reference to Provision for People with Mental Handicap and for People with Mental Illness*. London: Croom Helm.

Baker, P. M. (1983) The friendship process: a developmental model of interpersonal attraction. *Sociological Spectrum* **3**, 263–277.

Baldwin, S. (1981) *The financial consequences of disablement in children*. University of York: Department of Social Administration and Social Work. Social Policy Research Unit.

Barclay, P. (1982) *Social Workers: Their Role and Tasks*. National Institute for Social Work, London: Bedford Square Press.

Bardo, J. W. (1984) Sociospatial predictors of community satisfaction. *Journal of Social Psychology* **122**, 189–198.

Bayley, M. J. (1988) Normalisation or social role valorization – an adequate philosophy? In J. Hattersley and S. Baldwin (eds) *Social Science Perspectives*. London: Croom Helm.

Becker, S. and MacPherson, S. (1986). *Poor Clients – The Extent and Nature of Financial Poverty Amongst the Consumers of Social Work Services*. University of Nottingham: Benefits Research Unit, Dept. of Social Administration and Social Work.

Belle, D. (1982) The stress of caring: women as providers of social support. In L. Goldberger and S. Breznitz (eds) *Handbook of Stress: Theoretical and Clinical Aspects.* New York: Free Press.

Berscheid, E. and Walster, E. (1974) Physical attractiveness. In L. Berkowitz (ed.) *Advances in Experimental Social Psychology*, Vol. 7. New York: Academic Press.

Billings, A. G. and Moos, R. H. (1981) The role of coping responses and social resources in attenuating the stress of life events. *Journal of Behavioural Medicine* **4**, 139–157.

Boyce, W. T., Jensen, E. W., Cassel, J. C., Collier, A. M., Smith, A. H. and Ramey, C. T. (1977) Influence of life events and family routines on childhood respiratory tract illness. *Pediatrics* **60**, 609–615.

Braddock, D. and Heller, T. (1985) The closure of mental retardation institutions. II: Implications. *Mental Retardation* **23**, 222–229.

Bregman, S. (1985) Assertiveness training for mentally retarded adults. *Psychiatric Aspects of Mental Retardation Reviews* **4**, 43–48.

Brown, G. W. and Harris, T. (1978) *Social Origins of Depression.* London: Tavistock.

Brown, R. I. and Hughson, E. A. (1980) *Training of the Developmentally Handicapped Adult: A Practical Guide to Habilitation.* Springfield, Illinois: Charles C. Thomas.

Bruininks, R. H., Meyers, C. E., Sigford, B. B. and Lakin, K. C. (eds) (1981) *Deinstitutionalization and Community Adjustment of Mentally Retarded People.* Washington DC: American Association on Mental Deficiency, Monograph No. 4.

Buckle, J. (1984) *Mental Handicap Costs More.* London: Disablement Income Group Charitable Trust.

Burda, P. C., Vaux, A. and Schill, T. (1984) Social support resources: variations across sex and sex role. *Personality and Social Psychology Bulletin* **10**, 119–126.

Byrne, D. S., Harrison, S. P., Keithley, J. and McCarthy, P. (1986) *Housing and Health – The Relationship between Housing Conditions and the Health of Council Tenants.* Aldershot: Gower Publishing Co. Ltd.

Byrne, E. A. and Cunningham, C. C. (1985) The effects of mentally handicapped children on families: a conceptual review. *Journal of Child Psychology and Psychiatry* **26**, 847–866.

Campbell, A., Converse, P. E., and Rodgers, W. L. (1976) *The Quality of American Life.* New York: Russell Sage Foundation.

Card, H. (1983) What will happen when we've gone? *Community Care* **28**, 20–21.

Central Statistical Office (1983). *Social Trends 14*: A publication of the Government Statistical Service. London: HMSO.

Clark, G. R., Kivitz, M. S. and Rosen, M. (1968). *A Transitional Program for Institutionalized Adult Retarded.* Final Report. Pennsylvania: Elwyn Institute.

Cobb, H. V. (1972) *The Forecast of Fulfillment: A Review of Research on Predictive Assessment of the Adult Retarded for Social and Vocational Adjustment.* New York: Teachers College Press.

Cook, F., Skogan, W., Cook, T. and Antunes, G. (1978) Criminal victimization of the elderly: the physical and economic consequences. *The Gerontologist* **18**, 338–349.

Craft, A. and Craft M. (1979) *Handicapped Married Couples.* London: Routledge and Kegan Paul.

Dahman, D. C. (1983) Subjective assessments of neighbourhood quality by size of place. *Urban Studies* **20**, 31–45.

Dahman, D. C. (1985) Assessments of neighbourhood quality in metropolitan America. *Urban Affairs Quarterly* **20**, 511–535.

Davie, C. E., Hutt, S. J., Vincent, E. and Mason, M. (1982) *The Young Child at Home.* Windsor, Berks: NFER-Nelson.

Department of the Environment (1980) *Housing Requirements – A Guide to Information and Techniques.* London: HMSO.

Department of Health and Social Security (1971) *Better Services for the Mentally Handicapped* (CMND 4683). London: HMSO.

Department of Health and Social Security (1981) *Care in the Community: A Consultative Document on Moving Resources for Care in England*. London: DHSS.

Department of Health and Social Security Personal Social Services Local Authority Statistics (DHSSPSSLAS) (1977–82) *Homes and Hostels for the Mentally Ill and Mentally Handicapped at 31 March 1977–1982* (England, 6 volumes), A/F77/11-A/F83/11.

Department of Health and Social Security (1983) *Care in the Community and Joint Finance*. Circular HC (83) 6. London: DHSS.

Disabled Persons (Services, Consultation and Representation) Act 1986, London: HMSO.

Duncan, T. L. C. (1971) *Measuring household quality, CURS Occasional Paper, No. 20*, University of Birmingham.

Durward, L. (1981) *That's the Way the Money Goes*. London: The Disability Alliance.

Eastwood, L. (1987) Group home/landlady schemes: a case study. In N. Malin (ed.) *Reassessing Community Care: with Particular Reference to Provision for People with Mental Handicap and for People with Mental Illness*. London: Croom Helm.

Edgerton, R. B. (1967) *The Cloak of Competence: Stigma in the Lives of the Mentally Retarded*. Berkeley: University of California Press.

Edgerton, R. B. (1975). Issues relating to the quality of life among mentally retarded persons. In M. J. Begab and S. A. Richardson (eds) *The Mentally Retarded and Society: A Social Science Perspective*. Baltimore: University Park Press.

Edgerton, R. B. and Bercovici, S. M. (1976) The cloak of competence: years later. *American Journal of Mental Deficiency* 80, 485–497.

Edgerton, R. B., Bollinger, M. and Herr, B. (1984) The cloak of competence: after two decades. *American Journal of Mental Deficiency* 88, 345–351.

Emery, C. L., Watson, J. L., Watson, P. J., Thompson, D. M. and Biderman, M. D. (1985) Variables related to body–weight status of mentally retarded adults. *American Journal of Mental Deficiency* 90, 34–39.

Fernald, W. (1919) After-care study of the patients discharged from Waverley for a period of 25 years. *Ungraded* 5, 25–31.

Ferrara, D. M. (1979) Attitudes of parents of mentally retarded children toward normalization activities. *American Journal of Mental Deficiency* 84, 145–151.

Finch, J. (1984) It's great to have someone to talk to: the ethics and politics of interviewing women. In C. Bell and H. Roberts (eds) *Social Researching, Politics, Problems, Practice*. London: Routledge and Kegan Paul.

Fischer, C. T. and Wertz, F. J. (1979) Empirical phenomenological analyses of being criminally victimized. In A. Giorgi, R. Knowles and D. L. Smith (eds). *Duquesne Studies in Phenomenological Psychology*, vol. 3. Pittsburgh: Duquesne University Press.

Flanagan, J. C. (1978) A research approach to improving our quality of life. *American Psychologist* 33, 138–147.

Floor, L. D., Baxter, M. R. and Zisfain, L. (1975) A survey of marriages among previously institutionalized retardates. *Mental Retardation* 13, 33–37.

Florian, V. (1982) The meaning of work for physically disabled clients undergoing vocational rehabilitation. *International Journal of Rehabilitation Research* 5, 375–377.

Flynn, M. C. (1984) Community backlash, Parents Voice. *Journal of the Royal Society for Mentally Handicapped Children and Adults* 34, 16–17.

Flynn, M. C. (1985a) *A study of prediction in the community placements of adults who are mentally handicapped* (1983–86), Progress Report. Submission to the ESRC, September 1985.

Flynn, M. C. (1985b) Objectives and prognoses recorded in the case records of mentally handicapped adults living in their own homes. *British Journal of Social Work* **15**, 519–524.

Flynn, M. C. (1986a) Recording unstaffed community places in the DHSSPSSLAS: a study of the criteria used. *Mental Handicap* **14**, 52–53.

Flynn, M. C. (1986b) Adults who are mentally handicapped as consumers: issues and guidelines for interviewing. *Journal of Mental Deficiency Research* **30**, 369–377.

Flynn, M. C. (1986c) *A study of prediction in the community placements of adults who are mentally handicapped* (1983–86). Final report submitted to the ESRC.

Flynn, M. C. (1987) Independent living arrangements for adults who are mentally handicapped. In N. Malin (ed.) *Reassessing Community Care: with Particular Reference to Provision for People with Mental Handicap and for People with Mental Illness*. London: Croom Helm.

Flynn, M. C. and Knussen, C. (1986) What it means to be labelled 'mentally handicapped'. *Social Work Today* **16 June**, 11.

Flynn, M. C. and Saleem, J. K. (1986) Adults who are mentally handicapped and living with their parents: satisfaction and perceptions regarding their lives and circumstances. *Journal of Mental Deficiency Research* **30**, 379–387.

Flynn, M. C., Reeves, D. J., Whelan, E. and Speake, B. (1986) The development of a measure for determining the mentally handicapped adults' tolerance of rules and recognition of rights. *Journal of Practical Approaches to Developmental Handicap* **9**, 18–24.

Flynn, R. J. and Nitsch, K. E. (1980) Normalization: accomplishments to date and future priorities. In R. J. Flynn and K. E. Nitsch (eds) *Normalization, Social Integration and Community Services*. Baltimore: University Park Press.

Foss, G., Bostwick, D. and Harris, J. (1978) *Problems of mentally retarded young adults and obstacles to their rehabilitation: a study of consumers and service providers. Centre Paper No. 112*. Eugene: Rehabilitation Research and Training Centre in Mental Retardation, University of Oregon.

Fox, R. and Rotatori, A. F. (1982) Prevalence of obesity among mentally retarded adults. *American Journal of Mental Deficiency* **87**, 228–230.

Galster, G. C. and Hesser, G. W. (1981), Residential satisfaction – compositional and contextual correlates. *Environment and Behaviour* **13**, 735–758.

Ginsberg, Y. and Churchman, A. (1984) Housing satisfaction and intention to move: their explanatory variables. *Socio-Economic Planning Sciences* **18**, 425–431.

Gladstone, D. E. (1985) Disabled people and unemployment. *Social Policy and Administration* **19**, 101–111.

Goldstein, H. (1964) Social and occupational adjustment. In H. A. Stevens and R. Heber (eds) *Mental Retardation: A Review of Research*. Chicago: University of Chicago Press.

Gollay, E., Freedman, R., Wyngaarden, M. and Kurtz, N. R. (1978) *Coming Back: The Community Experiences of Deinstitutionalized Mentally Retarded People*. Cambridge, Mass.: Abt Associates.

Gore, S. (1978) The effect of social support in moderating the health consequences of unemployment. *Journal of Health and Social Behaviour* **19**, 157–165.

Gottlicb, B. H. (1985) Assessing and strengthening the impact of social support on mental health. *Social Work* **July–August**, 293–300.

Grossman, H. (1975) *A Manual on Classification*. Washington DC: American Association on Mental Deficiency.

Guess, D. (1984) Allowing the child greater participation in the educational process. Keynote address: *Fifth Annual Montana Symposium, Early Education and the Exceptional Child*. **April**, Billings, Montana.

Gurin, G., Veroff, J. and Feld, S. (1960) *Americans View Their Mental Health*. New York: Basic Books.

Haas, L. M. (1979) *The mentally retarded and the social context of fertility control*, Working Paper No. 9, Socio-Behavioral Group, University of California.

Heller, K., Rasmussen, B. R., Cook, J. R. and Wolosin, R. (1981) The effects of personal and social ties on satisfaction and perceived strain in changing neighbourhoods. *Journal of Community Psychology* **9**, 35–44.

Heller, T. (1984) Issues in adjustment of mentally retarded individuals to residential relocation. In N. R. Ellis and N. W. Bray (eds) *International Review of Research in Mental Retardation*, vol. 12. New York: Academic Press.

Hendrix, E. (1981) The fallacies of the concept of normalization. *Mental Retardation* **19**, 295–296.

Hill, B. and Bruininks, R. H. (1977) *Assessment of behavioural characteristics of people who are mentally retarded, developmental disabilities project on residential services and community adjustment*. Project Report No. 1, University of Minnesota.

Holbrook, R. C. and Mulhern, T. J. (1976) Alternative to walls. *Mental Retardation* **14**, 28–29.

House of Commons Social Services Committee, Session 1984–85 (1985) Second Report, *Community care with special reference to adult mentally ill and mentally handicapped people*. London: HMSO.

House, J. S. (1981) *Work Stress and Social Support*. Reading, Mass.: Addison-Wesley.

Hughes, M. and Gove, W. R. (1981) Living alone, social contact and psychological well being. *American Journal of Sociology* **87**, 48–74.

Independent Development Council for People with Mental Handicap (1981) *Response to 'Care in the Community': a DHSS Consultative Document on Moving Resources for Care in England*. London: IDC.

Iso-Ahola, S. E. (1980) *The Social Psychology of Leisure and Recreation*. Dubuque, Iowa: William C. Brown.

Iso-Ahola, S. E. and Allen, J. R. (1982) The dynamics of leisure motivation: the effects of outcome on leisure needs. *Research Quarterly for Exercise and Sport* **53**, 141–149.

James, N. (1984) A postscript to nursing. In C. Bell and H. Roberts (eds) *Social Researching, Politics, Problems, Practice*. London: Routledge and Kegan Paul.

Jay Committee (1979) *Report of The Committee of Enquiry into Mental Handicap Nursing and Care*. Cmnd 7468 I and II. London: HMSO.

Jenkins, R. (1984) Bringing it all back home: an anthropologist in Belfast. In C. Bell and H. Roberts (eds) *Social Researching, Politics, Problems, Practice*. London: Routledge and Kegan Paul.

Johnson, W. R. (1969) Sex education and the mentally retarded. *Journal of Sex Research* **5**, 179–185.

Johnson-Saylor, M. T. (1984) Unemployment and health: issues in primary care nursing practice. *Public Health Nursing* **1**, 74–84.

Johnston, D. F. (1981) Introduction. In D. F. Johnston (ed.) *Measurement of Subjective Phenomena*, Special Demographic Analyses. Washington: US Department of Commerce, Bureau of the Census.

Kabanoff, B. (1980) Work and nonwork: a review of models, methods and findings. *Psychological Bulletin* **88**, 60–77.

Kail, B. L. and Kleinman, P. H. (1985) Fear, crime, community organisation, and limitations on daily routines. *Urban Affairs Quarterly* **20**, 400–408.

Kelly, J. R. (1982) *Leisure*. Washington, Englewood Cliffs, NJ: Prentice Hall.

Kernan, K. T. and Koegal, P. (1980) *Employment experiences of community based mildly retarded adults*, Working Paper No. 14. Socio-Behavioral Group, University of California.

Kessler, R. C. and Essex, M. (1982) Marital status and depression: the importance of coping resources. *Social Forces* **61**, 484–507.

Kings Fund Centre (1980) *An Ordinary Life: Comprehensive Locally Based Residential Services for Mentally Handicapped People*. Project paper 24. London: Kings Fund.

Kleinman, M., Pearce, B. and Whitehead, C. (1985) *Housing: twenty-five popular fallacies. Discussion Paper Series 14*, Department of Land Economy, University of Cambridge.

Koegal, P. (1978) *The creation of incompetence: socialisation and mildly retarded persons, Working Paper No. 6*, Socio-Behavioral Group, University of California.

Ladewig, H. and McCann, G. C. (1980) Community satisfaction: theory and measurement. *Rural Sociology* **45**, 110–131.

Landesman Dwyer, S. (1981) Living in the community. *American Journal of Mental Deficiency* **87**, 34–39.

Latib, A., Conroy, J. and Hess, C. M. (1984) Family attitudes toward deinstitutionalisation. In N. R. Ellis and N. W. Bray (eds) *International Review of Mental Retardation*, vol. 12. New York: Academic Press.

Liang, J. and Sengstock, M. (1981) The risk of personal victimization among the aged. *Journal of Gerontology* **36**, 463–471.

Lin, N. and Dean, A. (1984) Social support and depression. *Social Psychiatry* **19**, 83–91.

Lin, N., Simeone, R. S., Ensel, W. M. and Kuo, W. (1979) Social support, stressful life events and illness: a model and empirical test. *Journal of Health and Social Behaviour* **20**, 108–119.

Luckman, A. L. (1986) *Should they all come out now?* Third year Project, Department of Psychology, University of Manchester.

Malin, N. (1983) *Group Homes for Mentally Handicapped People*. London: HMSO.

Malin, N. (ed.) (1987) *Reassessing Community Care: with Particular Reference to Provision for People with Mental Handicap and for People with Mental Illness*. London: Croom Helm.

Manpower Services Commission (1982) *Review of Assistance for Disabled People*. Sheffield: MSC.

Mattinson, J. (1970) *Marriage and Mental Handicap*. London: Duckworth.

McCarver, R. B. and Craig, E. M. (1974) Placement of the retarded in the community: prognosis and outcome. In N. R. Ellis (ed.) *International Review of Research in Mental Retardation*. New York: Academic Press.

McCord, W. T. (1983) The outcome of normalization: strengthened bonds between handicapped persons and their communities. *Education and Training of the Mentally Retarded* **18**, 153–157.

McKenna, C. L. (1986) *Self advocacy in the lives of people with mental handicaps*. Unpublished MPhil, University of Manchester.

Meyer, R. J. (1980) Attitudes of parents of institutionalized mentally retarded individuals toward deinstitutionalization. *American Journal of Mental Deficiency* **85**, 184–187.

Miller, E. J. and Gwynne, G. V. (1972) *A Life Apart: A Pilot Study of Residential Institutions for the Physically Handicapped and the Young Chronic Sick*. London: Tavistock Publications.

Miller, P. M. and Ingham, J. G. (1976) Friends, confidants and symptoms. *Social Psychiatry* **11**, 51–58.

Moen, M., Bogen, D. and Aanes, D. (1975) Follow-up of mentally retarded adults successfully placed in community group homes. *Hospital and Community Psychiatry* **26**, 754–756.

National Development Group for the Mentally Handicapped (1977) *Day Services for Mentally Handicapped Adults*. London: DHSS.

National Development Group for the Mentally Handicapped (1980) *Improving the Quality of Services for Mentally Handicapped People: A Checklist of Standards*. London: DHSS.

National Development Team for Mentally Handicapped People (1985) *Fourth Report, 1981–84*. London: HMSO.

Near, J. P., Rice, R. W. and Hunt, R. G. (1980) The relationship between work and non work domains: a review of empirical research. *Academy of Management Review* **5**, 415–429.

Nirje, B. (1969) The normalization principle and its human management implications. In R. B. Kugel and W. Wolfensberger (eds) *Changing Patterns in Residential Services for the Mentally Retarded*. Washington DC: President's Committee on Mental Retardation.

Oakley, A. (1981) Interviewing women: a contradiction in terms. In H. Roberts (ed.) *Doing Feminist Research*. London: Routledge and Kegan Paul.

Oliver, J. M. and Pomicter, C. (1981) Depression in automotive assembly-line workers as a function of unemployment variables. *American Journal of Community Psychology* **9**, 507–512.

Olson, D. H. and McCubbin, H. I. *et al.* (1983) *Families: What Makes Them Work*. Sage: Beverley Hills.

O'Neill, A. M. (1985) Normal and bright children of mentally retarded parents: the Huck Finn syndrome. *Child Psychiatry and Human Development* **15**, 255–268.

Payne, J. E. (1976) The deinstitutionalization backlash. *Mental Retardation* **3**, 43–45.

Pitceathly, A. S. and Chapman, J. W. (1985) Sexuality, marriage and parenthood of mentally retarded people. *International Journal for the Advancement of Counselling* **8**, 173–181.

Powell, T. H. and Ogle, P. A. (1985) *Brothers and Sisters – A Special Part of Exceptional Families*. Baltimore: Paul Brooks Publishing Co.

Purkis, A. and Hodson, P. (1982) *Housing and Community Care*. National Council for Voluntary Organisations. London: Bedford Square Press.

Race, D. (1987) Normalization: theory and practice. In N. Malin (ed.) *Reassessing Community Care: with Particular Reference to Provision for People with Mental Handicap and for People with Mental Illness*. London: Croom Helm.

Raynes, N. V., Sumpton, R. and Flynn, M. C. (1987) *Homes for Mentally Handicapped People*. London: Associated Press.

Rhoades, C. and Browning, P. (1977) Normalization at what price? *Mental Retardation* **15**, 24.

Richardson, A. and Ritchie, J. (1986) *Making the Break: Parents' Views about Adults with a Mental Handicap Leaving the Parental Home*. London: King's Fund Publishing Office, Policy Studies Institute and Social and Community Planning Research.

Richardson, S. A., Koller, H., Katz, M. and McLaren, J. (1980) Seizures and epilepsy in a mentally retarded population over the first 22 years of life. *Applied Research in Mental Retardation* **1**, 123–138.

Richardson, S. A., Koller, H. and Katz, M. (1985) Appearance and mental retardation: some first steps in the development and application of a measure. *American Journal of Mental Deficiency* **89**, 475–484.

Robinson, R., O'Sullivan, T. and Le Grand, J. (1985) Inequality and housing. *Urban Studies* **22**, 249–256.

Rose, A. (1985) Housing and the community. *Canadian Journal of Public Health* **76**, 71–73.

Rotatori, A. F., Switzky, H. N. and Fox, R. (1983) Obesity in mentally retarded, psychiatric and non-handicapped individuals: a learning and biological disability. In K. D. Gadow and I. Bialer (eds) *Advances in Learning and Behavioural Disabilities*, vol. 2. Greenwich, Conn.: JAI Press.

Rumsey, N. J., Bull, R. and Gahagan, D. (1982) The effect of facial disfigurement on the proxemic behaviour of the general public. *Journal of Applied Social Psychology* **12**, 137–150.

Rutter, M. (1981) Stress, coping and development: some issues and some questions. *Journal of Child Psychology and Psychiatry* **22**, 323–356.

Schalock, R. L., Harper, R. S. and Carver, G. (1981) Independent living placement: five years later. *American Journal of Mental Deficiency* **86**, 170–177.

Sherrill, C. (1980) Posture training as a means of normalization. *Mental Retardation* **18**, 135–138.

Sigelman, C. K., Budd, E. C., Winer, J. L., Schoenrock, C. J. and Martin, P. W. (1982) Evaluating alternative techniques of questioning mentally retarded persons. *American Journal of Mental Deficiency* **86**, 511–518.

Sikking, M. (1986) Co-ops with a difference: worker co-ops for people with special needs. London: ICOM Co-Publication.

Staines, G. L. (1980) Spillover versus compensation: a review of the literature on the relationship between work and non work. *Human Relations* **33**, 111–129.

Starker, J. (1986) Methodological and conceptual issues in research on social support. *Hospital and Community Psychiatry* **37**, 485–490.

Stokes, J. P. and Wilson, D. G. (1984) The inventory of socially supportive behaviours: dimensionality, prediction and gender differences. *American Journal of Community Psychology* **12**, 53–69.

Sullivan, D. R. (1972) Maslow's hierarchy of needs in relation to employment. *Journal of Employment Counseling* **9**, 94–95.

Sumpton, R., Flynn, M. and Raynes, N. (1986) Case records of mentally handicapped people living in a variety of settings: some observations and recommendations. *Research, Policy and Planning* Journal of the Social Services Research Group **4**, 38–42.

Surtees, P. G. (1980) Social support, residual adversity and depressive outcome. *Social Psychiatry* **15**, 71–80.

Taylor, R. and Ford, G. (1983) Inequalities in old age: an examination of age, sex and class differences in a sample of community elderly. *Ageing and Society* **3**, 183–208.

Tizard, J. (1965) Longitudinal and follow-up studies. In A. M. Clarke and A. D. B. Clarke (eds) *Mental Deficiency: The Changing Outlook*, 2nd edition. London: Methuen.

Towell, D. (ed.) (1988) *An Ordinary Life in Practice*. London: King Edwards Hospital Fund for London.

Townsend, P. (1979) *Poverty in the United Kingdom. A Survey of Household Resources and Standards of Living*. Harmondsworth: Penguin Books.

Turnbull, A. P. and Turnbull, H. R. (1985) Developing independence. *Journal of Adolescent Health Care* **6**, 108–119.

United Nations (1971) *Declaration on the Rights of Mentally Retarded Persons, General Assembly Resolution 2865 (XXVI) of 20 December, 1971*. Geneva: United Nations.

Vash, C. L. (1982) Women and employment. In L. G. Perlman and K. C. Arneson (eds) *Women and Rehabilitation of Disabled Persons: A report of the 6th Mary E. Switzer Memorial Seminar, Virginia*. Virginia: National Rehabilitation Association.

Walker, A. (1981) Disability and income. In A. Walker and P. Townsend (eds) *Disability in Britain*. Oxford: Martin Robertson.

Wertheimer, A. (1983) *Leisure: A CMH Discussion Paper*. London: CMH.

Wertheimer, A. (1986) *Hospital Closures in the Eighties*. London: Campaign for People with Mental Handicaps.

Whelan, E. and Speake, B. (1981) *Getting to Work*. London: Souvenir Press.

Whittemore, R. D. and Koegel, P. (1978) *Loving alone is not helpful: Sexuality and social context among the mildly retarded*, Working Paper No. 7, Socio-Behavioral Group, University of California.

Wilkin, D. (1979) *Caring for the Mentally Handicapped Child*. London: Croom Helm.

Willer, B. and Intagliata, J. (1984) An overview of the social policy of deinstitutionalization. In N. R. Ellis and N. Bray (eds) *International Review of Research in Mental Retardation*. New York: Academic Press.

Williams, A., Ware, J. E. and Donald, C. A. (1981) A model of mental health, life events and social supports applicable to general populations. *Journal of Health and Social Behavior* **22**, 324–336.

Williams, N. J., Sewel, J. and Twine, F. (1986) Council house allocation and tenant incomes. *Area* **18**, 131–140.

Winik, L. (1982) *Mildly retarded adults as parents: a description of the parenting practices of two mildly retarded couples. Working Paper No. 22*, Socio-Behavioral Group, University of California.

Wolfensberger, W. (1972) *The Principle of Normalization in Human Services*. Toronto: National Institute of Mental Retardation.

Wolfensberger, W. (1983) Social role valorization: a proposed new term for the principle of normalization. *Mental Retardation* **21**, 234–239.

Appendix 1

The information presented here is derived from Pearson Product Moment Correlations. It is evident that, in general, the people who need support receive it.

Money management
Help with the payment of bills and managing finances is more likely to be given to people who:

- have expressed dissatisfaction with their money management ($r = -0.19$, $p = 0.04$, $N = 80$);
- have, or have had debts ($r = -0.30$, $p = 0.005$, $N = 74$);
- are poor at managing money ($r = -0.32$, $p = 0.002$, $N = 84$);
- receive benefits rather than a wage ($r = -0.022$, $p = 0.02$, $N = 84$); and
- are poor at decision-making ($r = -0.17$, $p = 0.06$, $N = 84$).

Health and personal hygiene
Support with health and hygiene is more likely to be given to people who:

- have medical problems and who need reminders to keep clean ($r = -0.33$, $p = 0.0001$, $N = 82$);
- have poor self-care skills ($r = -0.38$, $p = 0.001$, $N = 85$); and
- have communication problems ($r = -0.21$, $p = 0.03$, $N = 85$).

Home and household
The people who receive support regarding their homes are those who:

- are dissatisfied with their homes ($r = -0.10$, $p = 0.04$, $N = 75$);
- live in poor quality homes ($r = -0.16$, $p = 0.077$, $N = 80$); and
- live in flats rather than houses ($r = -0.24$, $p = 0.01$, $N = 84$).

Interpersonal issues
Support in the interpersonal sphere is more likely to be given to people who:

- have few relationships ($r = -0.33$, $p = 0.002$, $N = 74$);
- are dissatisfied with their limited social lives ($r = -0.23$, $p = 0.027$, $N = 69$); and
- are poor at handling relationships ($r = -0.44$, $p = 0.001$, $N = 73$).

Daily and leisure activities
In terms of the effectiveness of this support, the people who are most likely to receive assistance with their daily activities are people who:

- have a structured day ($r = 0.17$, $p = 0.06$, $N = 86$).

In respect of leisure, the people who are most likely to receive help in this area are those who:

- are dissatisfied with their leisure ($r = -0.31$, $p = 0.004$, $N = 78$); and
- are receiving support regarding their daily activities ($r = 0.46$, $p = 0.001$, $N = 76$).

Appendix 2

Table A *Multiple regression on index of concern*

Independent variables	Beta coefficients*	*p*	Cumulative %
Health and hygiene weight problem/poor diet; depression; general deterioration observed; neglectful of personal hygiene; concern expressed by medical services; hair and clothing dirty; drinking problem; smoking heavily.	0.612	<0.0001	46
Sex	0.201	0.034	50

* The beta coefficient is a measure of the direct impact of the independent variable onto the dependent variable when preceding variables are held constant

p: probability level

Cumulative % is the percentage of variance explained when the variable entered the regression equation.

Table B *Multiple regression on index of debts*

Independent variables	Beta coefficients	*p*	Cumulative %
Victimisation mugging/physical abuse; home and property damaged; property stolen/financially 'milked'; intimidation from neighbours; intimidation from children; and fears neighbours/local children	0.387	<0.0001	24
Household routines for money; cooking; laundry; shopping; and cleaning	0.241	0.023	34
Year of birth	0.294*N*	0.007	39
Daily activity activity is structured versus activity is unstructured	0.329	0.004	44
Income salary; or benefits	0.235*N*	0.039	48

N denotes a negative association

Table C   *Multiple regression on index of satisfaction with money management*

Independent variables	Beta coefficients	p	Cumulative %
Skills re interpersonal issues skills of handling relationship with man/ woman friend; and skills of handling interpersonal relationships	0.377	0.002	26
Satisfaction with daily activity desire to change daily activity	0.334	0.005	36

Table D   *Multiple regression on index of cleanliness of people's homes*

Independent variables	Beta coefficients	p	Cumulative %
Household facilities (see Table K)	0.502	<0.0001	24
Avoidance avoids specialist services/personnel; or does not avoid.	0.244	0.030	30

Table E   *Multiple regression on index of health and hygiene problems*

Independent variables	Beta coefficients	p	Cumulative %
Environment (see Table L)	0.309	0.010	30
Appearance (see Table L)	0.211	0.042	37
State of repair of home	0.265	0.021	42
Satisfaction with daily activity desire to change this	0.230	0.033	43

Table F   *Multiple regression on index of satisfaction with daily activity*

Independent variables	Beta coefficients	p	Cumulative %
Household routines (see Table B)	0.353	0.003	25
Avoidance avoids specific services/personnel; or does not avoid	0.266	0.021	33
Home lives in flat; or lives in house	0.229	0.041	38

Table G   *Multiple regression on index of having positive relationships with people*

Independent variables	Beta coefficients	p	Cumulative %
Victimisation (see Table B)	0.332	<0.0001	29
Length of time in own home/tenancy	0.417N	0.000	41
Sex	0.424	0.000	54
Skills re interpersonal issues (see Table C)	0.279	0.001	65
Avoidance avoids specialist services/personnel; does not avoid	0.180	0.032	68

N denotes a negative association

Table H   *Multiple regression on index of satisfaction with household tasks*

Independent variables	Beta coefficients	p	Cumulative %
Total number of tenancies	0.363N	0.002	15
Skills re interpersonal issues (see Table C)	0.298	0.007	22

N denotes a negative association

Table I   *Multiple regression on index of leisure satisfaction*

Independent variables	Beta coefficients	p	Cumulative %
Household facilities (see Table K)	0.236	0.059	6
Medical condition visual, hearing and heart problems; epilepsy; mental illness, mobility; metabolic, respiratory and/or gastrointestinal problems	0.264N	0.042	10
Daily activity daily activity is structured; or daily activity is unstructured	0.236	0.068	16

N denotes a negative association

Table J   *Multiple regression on index of satisfaction with interpersonal relations*

Independent variables	Beta coefficients	*p*	Cumulative %
Victimisation (see Table B)	0.515	<0.0001	33
Skills re interpersonal issues (see Table C)	0.216	0.045	39
Daily activity daily activity is structured; or daily activity is unstructured	0.188	0.072	43

Table K   *Multiple regression on index of home satisfaction*

Independent variables	Beta coefficients	*p*	Cumulative %
Victimisation (see Table B)	0.663	<0.0001	51
Household facilities TV; radio; fridge; washing machine; vacuum cleaner; telephone; central heating; adequate seating; and proportion of rooms heated in winter	0.328	0.001	59
State of repair of home rising damp; damp walls/ceilings; loose brickwork; badly fitting windows; and broken floorboards	0.307	0.003	62
Total number of tenancies	0.200*N*	0.037	66
Living situation lives alone; or lives with others	0.157*N*	0.053	68

N denotes a negative association

Table L   *Multiple regression on index of victimisation*

Independent variables	Beta coefficients	*p*	Cumulative %
Environment proximity of disused houses; of uncollected rubbish; of graffiti; density of local traffic; rateable value of property; walking time to local phone, launderette and food store	0.419	<0.0001	24
Appearance height; size; unusual features; facial asymmetry; facial twitch; prosthesis; physical handicaps; unusual posture; unusual gait; rocking; odd mannerisms; clothes bizarre, inappropriate and/or poorly cared for	0.241	0.032	30
Year of birth	0.206*N*	0.064	34

N denotes a negative association

Table M *Multiple regression on index of success*

Independent variables	Beta coefficients	p	Cumulative %
Debts	0.289	0.005	38
Satisfaction with household tasks with money management; cooking; laundry; shopping and cleaning	0.237	0.049	53
Environment (see Table L)	0.302	0.002	59
Satisfaction with money management	0.246	0.040	63

Name Index

Subject Index